# AMERICA FIRST

# AMERICA FIRST

## VARIOUS,
## JASPER LEONIDAS MCBRIEN

ISBN: 978-93-89679-83-0

Published:                    -

LECTOR HOUSE LLP
E-MAIL: lectorpublishing@gmail.com

AMERICA FIRST

# AMERICA FIRST
## PATRIOTIC READINGS

### EDITED BY

### JASPER L. MCBRIEN, A. M.

FORMER STATE SUPERINTENDENT OF PUBLIC INSTRUCTION
OF NEBRASKA AND NOW SCHOOL EXTENSION
SPECIALIST FOR THE UNITED STATES BUREAU
OF EDUCATION, WASHINGTON, D. C.

# FOREWORD

America First was the central thought in President Wilson's address to the Daughters of the American Revolution on the twenty-fifth anniversary of their organization—their Silver Jubilee—in Washington, D. C., October 11, 1915. The president declared in this address that all citizens should make it plain whether their sympathies for foreign countries come before their love of the United States, or whether they are for America first, last, and all the time. He asserted, also, that our people need all of their patriotism in this confusion of tongues in which we find ourselves over the European war.

The press throughout the country has taken up the thought of the President and, seconded by the efforts of the Bureau of Education, has done loyal work in making "America First" our national slogan. This is all good so far as it goes—especially among the adult population, many of whom must be educated, if educated at all, on the run. But the rising generation, both native-born and foreign, to get the full meaning of this slogan in its far-reaching significance, must have time for study and reflection along patriotic lines. There must be the right material on which the American youth may settle their thoughts for a definite end in patriotism if our country is to have a new birth of freedom and if "this government of the people, by the people, and for the people is not to perish from the earth." The prime and vital service of amalgamating into one homogeneous body the children alike of those who are born here and of those who come here from so many different lands must be rendered this Republic by the school teachers of America.

The purpose of this book is to furnish the teachers and pupils of our country, material with which the idea of true Americanism may be developed until "America First" shall become the slogan of every man, woman, and child in the United States.

# CONTENTS

## POETRY OF PATRIOTISM

# ACKNOWLEDGMENTS

Acknowledgments for permission to use copyrighted and other valuable material in this volume are hereby tendered to authors and publishers as follows:

To President Woodrow Wilson for his three addresses "America First," "The Meaning of the Flag," and "Neutrality Proclamation."

To Secretary Franklin K. Lane for his speech on "The Makers of the Flag."

To William Jennings Bryan and his publishers, Funk and Wagnalls Company, New York and London, for extracts from his address on "The Patriotism of Peace."

To Archbishop Ireland for extracts from his address on "The Duty and Value of Patriotism."

To George L. Schuman and Company, publishers of *Modern Eloquence*, Chicago, for the following extracts and addresses: "Our Country," by William McKinley; "Our Reunited Country," by Clark Howell; "The Blue and the Gray," by Henry Cabot Lodge; "A Reminiscence of Gettysburg," by John B. Gordon; "The New South," by Henry W. Grady; and "The Hollander as an American," by Theodore Roosevelt.

To A. C. Butters for the address on "Washington," by John W. Daniel, from *Modern Eloquence* published by George L. Schuman and Company.

To Henry Watterson, Louisville, Kentucky, for the extracts from his lecture on Abraham Lincoln.

To E. Benjamin Andrews and to his publishers, Fords, Howard and Hulbert, for the extracts from his lecture on Robert E. Lee.

To J. B. Lippincott Company, Philadelphia, for the poem by Thomas Buchanan Read, "The Rising in 1776."

To Charles Scribner's Sons, New York, for the poem by Henry van Dyke, "America for Me," and also for the extract from the poem "Wanted," by J. G. Holland.

To The Bobbs-Merrill Company, Indianapolis, for the poem by James Whitcomb Riley, "The Name of Old Glory."

To Henry Holcomb Bennett for his poem entitled, "The Flag Goes By."

To Christopher Sower Company, Philadelphia, for the poem by Edward Brooks, entitled "Be a Woman."

The selections from the poems of Ralph Waldo Emerson, Henry Wadsworth

Longfellow, James Russell Lowell, and Bayard Taylor are used by permission of and special arrangement with Houghton Mifflin Company, the authorized publishers of the works of those authors.

The thanks of the author are also extended to Nelson Warner, Katherine M. Cook, Mrs. L. R. Caldwell, Belvia Cuzzort, W. R. Hood, and Dr. Stephen B. Weeks of the Bureau of Education, for valuable assistance in the compilation of this work.

# THE CONTINENTAL CONGRESS
# A DRAMATIZATION

*Jasper L. McBrien*

SIGNING THE DECLARATION

# INTRODUCTION

This dramatization of the Continental Congress portrays the spirit of the times during the period of the American Revolution. It deals principally with the debates for and against the Declaration of Independence; it is a summary of the grievances, struggles, sacrifices, and victories of the colonies from the enactment of the obnoxious Stamp Act by the British Parliament to the resignation of George Washington as commander-in-chief of the American army.

In the construction of a drama covering such a heroic period and relating to events so momentous, all of which must pass in review before us within an hour and a half's time, it is necessary to exercise a certain dramatic license. The historical literalist, like the scriptural literalist, makes the letter kill the spirit of the truth. After all, it is not the dry facts, dates, and mechanics of history that are of greatest importance; it is the fundamental principles, causes, and effects underlying the events as well as the spirit of the times, that are of first consideration.

Any modification of historical fact in this dramatization has been made only to give a fuller meaning to the great facts of history touched upon therein. It is the period of the American Revolution that is to be portrayed, as already stated—not alone those memorable days of June and July, 1776, during which the debates on the Declaration of Independence took place. For example, Patrick Henry was a member of the First and the Second Continental Congress, though not a member at the time the Declaration of Independence was debated, Washington was a member of the First Continental Congress, but Jefferson was not. Congress was a changing body in its membership then as is our Congress to-day.

Jefferson declares that Patrick Henry was the man who put the ball of the American Revolution in motion. Not to give Henry a place in this dramatization would be like the play of "Hamlet" with Hamlet left out.

It must be remembered that no record was made of the debates in the Continental Congress as is done verbatim by expert reporters in Congress to-day and published in the Congressional Record. Therefore, the speeches herein have been adapted from such sources as Paine's "Separation of Britain and America," Webster's "Supposed Speech of John Adams," "Wirt's Supposed Speech of Patrick Henry," Alexander H. Stephens's "Corner Stone Speech," Webster's "Supposed Speech of Opposition to Independence," and Sumner's "True Grandeur of Nations." The dialogue between Jefferson and Adams is taken from a letter of John Adams to Timothy Pickering, dated August 6, 1822. The speeches of Stephens and Sumner are paraphrased to suit the times to which they are here applied.

Great care has been exercised to place each of the leading characters in these debates on the side in which he *at that time* conscientiously believed. In the roll call in this drama on the vote for independence, the history of each colony has been thoroughly studied so as to bring out the changed attitude of the people of the various colonies toward independence, as well as of certain members of the Continental Congress on this question.

The scenes of Washington and his army just before the battle of Long Island, the tableau of The Spirit of '76, and Washington's resignation as commander-in-chief of the army, are introduced not alone for their psychological effect on the dramatization proper, but for their own worth in teaching patriotism.

With twenty-nine leading characters the dramatization can be well staged. But if fifty-five characters are available—the number who signed the Declaration, and if there is room for so many, so much the better, except as the number of performers is increased there will be an additional expense for costumes.[1] It may be given as a reading lesson without costumes; it may be given so as a drama; but it is a greater success given in costumes.

Those who take part in this dramatization should be costumed as nearly like the characters they represent as possible. As a rule, wigs can be rented for this purpose at a reasonable cost, and it will not be difficult to dress in the style of the Revolutionary period—buckle shoes, silk stockings, knee pants, ruffled shirt, and the conventional coat of the time.

The same freedom must be permitted and exercised in carrying out this dramatization, that marked the actors in the Continental Congress itself in its stormy debates and noisy sessions. Immediately following the close of each speech there should be a clamor for recognition on the part of the delegates, but the president will be careful to recognize the proper person so as to make the play move without any hitch. As each speaker proceeds there should be a reasonable number of interruptions by applause or dissenting voices so as to play both sides as strongly as possible.

The parliamentary procedure must not be followed too strictly or it will kill the interest in the play on the part of the public. It must be given with dispatch and dramatic effect to make a happy hit.

These debates may be considered as an oratorical contest with prizes awarded accordingly if so desired. It adds interest to the work.

It is hard to tell in which years of school work it is best to give this dramatization—whether in the grammar grades, in the high school, or in the college, for it is within the understanding of grammar grade boys; it is not too elementary for young men in the high school; and it is profound enough for the best thought and the best efforts of college students. If given by grammar school boys and high school young men, it will have a wholesome influence in training for a better citizenship at an opportune time. If presented by college, university, and normal school students it will give those who are fitting themselves for teaching a valuable

[1] In small schools where there are not enough large boys to represent all the characters, those who represent members of the Continental Congress can become members of Washington's army, etc., for the other scenes.

lesson in methods. If it were given by every grammar school, high school, college, university and normal school, on every Chautauqua platform, and by every patriotic society in the United States on Washington's Birthday and other patriotic occasions, and then repeated on the Fourth of July every year for the next decade it would do much towards combating that dangerous "aggressive hyphenated Americanism," that has sprung up in our country and whose baneful effects it will take much earnest teaching to obliterate. When all native-born children of foreign parentage, and when all citizens of foreign birth know the story of the struggle and sacrifice by which our country rose to her proud station it will make them feel "that they are Americans among Americans; that they are part of America and have a share and a duty toward American institutions." May it also cause those native-born Americans who have become luke-warm in their love of country, careless of its honor, and negligent in its defense to awake to their duty with a spirit to do their duty before it is too late. May it make of every one of us a truer American "by being wholly and without reserve, and without divided allegiance, and with emphatic repudiation of the entire principle of 'dual nationality,' an American citizen and nothing else."

*In their ragged regimentals*
*Stood the old Continentals,*
*Yielding not,*
*When the grenadiers were lunging.*
*And like hail fell the plunging*
*Cannon shot;*
*When the files*
*Of the isles,*
*From the smoky night encampment, bore the banner of the rampant*
*Unicorn;*
*And grummer, grummer, grummer, rolled the roll of the drummer*
*Through the morn!*

TABLEAU—THE SBPIRIT OF SEVENTY-SIX

# CAST OF CHARACTERS



| FOR THE DECLARATION | AGAINST THE DECLARATION |
|---|---|
| John Hancock, *President* | Edward Rutledge |
| Richard Henry Lee | John Dickinson |
| John Adams | George Walton |
| Roger Sherman | Robert Morris |
| Benjamin Franklin | |
| Samuel Adams | |
| Joseph Hewes | |
| Patrick Henry | |
| Thomas Jefferson | |

Charles Thomson, *Secretary*

## OTHER MEMBERS OF THE CONGRESS

| | |
|---|---|
| Josiah Bartlett | Oliver Wolcott |
| Stephen Hopkins | Elbridge Gerry |
| William Floyd | William Hooper |
| Charles Carroll of Carrollton | Benjamin Rush |
| Samuel Chase | Richard Stockton |
| Benjamin Harrison | Thomas McKean |
| Lyman Hall | Caesar Rodney |

## ADDITIONAL CHARACTERS

General Washington and his Army

Fifer  
Drummer  Leading the Army in "The Spirit of  
Little Boy '76"

# THE CONTINENTAL CONGRESS
## ACT I.



*Scene I.—Congress assembled; John Hancock in the chair as president;
his keynote speech.*

John Hancock.[2] Gentlemen of the Continental Congress:—I thank you for
the signal honor you have conferred on me in making me your presiding officer.
I am glad to see so many Colonies represented in this Congress. Let us show the
nations of the old world what the people of the new world will do when left to
themselves, to their own unbiased good sense, and to their own true interests. On
us depend the destinies of our country—the fate of three millions of people, and of
the countless millions of our posterity. Matchless is our opportunity—matchless
also is our responsibility! May the God of nations guide us in our deliberations
and in our actions.

Everything that is right or natural pleads for separation. The blood of the slain,
the weeping voice of Nature cries, "'Tis time to part." Even the distance at which
the Almighty hath placed England and America, is a strong and natural proof that
the authority of the one over the other was never the design of Heaven. The time,
likewise, at which the continent was discovered, adds weight to the argument, and
the manner in which it was peopled, increases the force of it. The Reformation was
preceded by the discovery of America, as if the Almighty graciously meant to open
a sanctuary to the persecuted in future years, when home should afford neither
friendship nor safety.

The authority of Great Britain over this continent is a form of government
which sooner or later must have an end: and a serious mind can draw no true
pleasure by looking forward, under the painful and positive conviction that what
he calls "the present constitution" is merely temporary. As parents, we can have
no joy, knowing that this government is not sufficiently lasting to insure anything
which we may bequeath to posterity; and by a plain method of argument, as we
are running the next generation into debt, we ought to do the work of it, otherwise
we use them meanly and pitifully. In order to discover the line of our duty rightly,
we should take our children by the hand, and fix our station a few years farther
into life; that eminence will present a prospect which a few present fears and prejudices conceal from our sight.

Though I would carefully avoid giving unnecessary offense, yet I am inclined

_______________

[2] This speech is adapted from Paine's "Separation of Britain and America."

to believe that all those who espouse the doctrine of reconciliation may be included within the following descriptions: Interested men, who are not to be trusted; weak men, who cannot see; prejudiced men, who will not see; and a certain set of moderate men, who think better of the European world than it deserves: and this last class, by an ill-judged deliberation, will be the cause of more calamities to this continent than all the other three.

It is the good fortune of many to live distant from the scene of sorrow; the evil is not sufficiently brought to their doors to make them feel the precariousness with which all American property is possessed. But let our imaginations transport us a few moments to Boston; that seat of wretchedness will teach us wisdom, and instruct us forever to renounce a power in whom we can have no trust. The inhabitants of that unfortunate city, who but a few months ago were in ease and affluence, have no other alternative than to stay and starve, or turn out to beg. Endangered by the fire of their friends if they continue within the city, and plundered by the soldiery if they leave it. In their present situation they are prisoners without hope of redemption, and in a general attack for their relief they would be exposed to the fury of both armies.

Men of passive tempers look somewhat lightly over the offenses of Britain, and, still hoping for the best, are apt to call out, "Come, come, we shall be friends again for all this." But examine the passions and feelings of mankind, bring the doctrine of reconciliation to the touchstone of nature, and then tell me whether you can hereafter love, honor, and faithfully serve the power that hath carried fire and sword into your land? If you cannot do all these, then are you deceiving yourselves, and by your delay bringing ruin upon your posterity. Your future connection with Britain, whom you can neither love nor honor, will be forced and unnatural, and being formed only on the plan of present convenience, will in a little time fall into a relapse more wretched than the first. But if you say you can still pass the violations over, then I ask, hath your house been burnt? Hath your property been destroyed before your face? Are your wife and children destitute of a bed to lie on, or bread to live on? Have you lost a parent or a child by their hands, and yourself the ruined and wretched survivor? If you have not, then are you not a judge of those who have. But if you have, and can still shake hands with the murderers, then are you unworthy the name of husband, father, friend or lover, and, whatever may be your rank or title in life, you have the heart of a coward and the spirit of a sycophant.

Gentlemen of the First American Congress, in the name of Equality, Fraternity and Liberty, I welcome you to this council. What is your pleasure, gentlemen?

RICHARD HENRY LEE. Mr. President:—I wish to move the adoption of the following resolution: "Resolved, that these united colonies are, and of right ought to be free and independent states; that they are absolved from all allegiance to the British crown, and that all political connection between them and the state of Great Britain is, and ought to be, totally dissolved."

JOHN ADAMS. Mr. President:—I second the motion.

JOHN HANCOCK. Gentlemen of the Continental Congress, you have heard the motion of Mr. Richard Henry Lee, of Virginia, for immediate and absolute independence. Are there any remarks?

RICHARD HENRY LEE. Mr. President and Gentlemen of the Continental Congress:—Why do we delay? Why still deliberate? Let this happy day give birth to an American republic. Let her arise, not to devastate and to conquer, but to reëstablish the reign of peace and law. The eyes of Europe are fixed upon us. She demands of us a living example of freedom that may exhibit a contrast in the felicity of the citizen to the ever increasing tyranny which devastates her polluted shores. She invites us to prepare an asylum where the unhappy may find solace and the persecuted repose. She entreats us to cultivate a propitious soil where that generous plant of liberty, which first sprang and grew in England, but is now withered by the blasts of tyranny may revive and flourish, sheltering under its salubrious shade all the unfortunate of the human race. If we are not this day wanting in our duty to our country, the names of the American legislators of 1776 will be placed by posterity at the side of Theseus, of Lycurgus, of Romulus, of Numa, of the three Williams of Nassau and of all those whose memory has been and forever will be, dear to virtuous men and good citizens.[3]

*(At the close of Mr. Lee's brief speech there is a clamor for recognition.*
*John Adams is recognized.)*

JOHN ADAMS. Mr. President:—I move that a committee of five be selected by ballot to draft a Declaration representing the views of these united colonies.

BENJAMIN FRANKLIN. Mr. President:—I second the motion.

JOHN HANCOCK. Gentlemen of the Continental Congress:—The motion has been made and seconded that a committee of five be selected by ballot to draft a proper Declaration representing the views of these united colonies. You have heard the motion, are there any remarks? (*Calls for the question.*)

As many as favor this motion make it known by saying "aye" (*ayes respond*); contrary, "no" (*noes respond*). The ayes seem to have it, the ayes have it, and the motion is carried.

Gentlemen of the Continental Congress, I shall appoint Benjamin Rush of Pennsylvania, Samuel Chase of Maryland, and Edward Rutledge of South Carolina as tellers for this election and they will wait upon you for your ballots for the committee. Please write the names of the five men whom you wish to serve on this committee, on your ballot and deposit the same in the hat when passed.

*(Ballots are gathered by the tellers who report the result to the president*
*of the Congress.)*

Gentlemen of the Continental Congress:—By your ballots you have selected the following persons as the committee of five to draft the Declaration as already ordered—Thomas Jefferson of Virginia, John Adams of Massachusetts, Benjamin Franklin of Pennsylvania, Roger Sherman of Connecticut, and Robert R. Livingston of New York. Gentlemen, what is your further pleasure?

---

[3] Adapted from Wirt's supposed speech of Lee.

Samuel Adams. Mr. President:—I move that the Congress do now take a recess until to-morrow morning at 10 o'clock to give the committee just appointed time in which to prepare the Declaration ordered.

Joseph Hewes. Mr. President:—I second the motion which Mr. Adams has offered.

John Hancock. Gentlemen of the Congress:—It has been moved and seconded that this Congress take a recess until to-morrow morning at 10 o'clock in order to give the committee just appointed time in which to prepare a proper Declaration. You have heard the motion, are there any remarks? (*Calls for question.*)

As many as favor the motion make it known by saying "aye" (*ayes respond*); contrary, "no" (*noes respond*). The ayes seem to have it, the ayes have it, and this Congress will take a recess until to-morrow morning at 10 o'clock.

CURTAIN

# ACT II.

## *Scene I.—Meeting of the Committee of Five. Livingston absent.*

Benjamin Franklin. Gentlemen of the Committee, I move that Thomas Jefferson and John Adams be appointed as a sub-committee of this Committee of Five to draft the Declaration ordered by the Continental Congress.

Roger Sherman. I second the motion.

Benjamin Franklin. Gentlemen, you have heard the motion. As many as favor the same make it known by saying "aye."

> *(Mr. Jefferson and Mr. Adams are silent while Mr. Sherman and Mr.*
> *Franklin vote aye.)*

The ayes seem to have it, the ayes have it, and Mr. Jefferson and Mr. Adams are elected.

John Adams. Gentlemen, it seems to me you have taken snap judgment on Mr. Jefferson and myself.

Thomas Jefferson. Yes, gentlemen, you have.

Benjamin Franklin. The committee has so ordered and as Congress itself gave Mr. Jefferson the highest number of votes and Mr. Adams the next highest number in the selection of this committee, I am sure that Congress will be highly pleased at our having selected you for this great work. We also feel that we should congratulate ourselves upon the choice we have made.

John Adams. Thank you, gentlemen, for the compliment.

Thomas Jefferson. I join Mr. Adams in thanking you, gentlemen, for the confidence you have in us.

Roger Sherman. Gentlemen of the committee, I move that we take a recess until to-night so as to give the sub-committee time to prepare the Declaration.

Mr. Adams. I second the motion.

Mr. Franklin. As many as favor the motion make it known by saying "aye" *(ayes respond)*. The ayes seem to have it, the ayes have it, and the committee will take a recess until eight o'clock to-night.

> *(Mr. Franklin and Mr. Sherman leave Mr. Adams and Mr. Jefferson to*
> *themselves to deliberate over the Declaration.)*

Mr. Jefferson. Mr. Adams, I suggest that you make the draft of this Declaration.

Mr. Adams. I will not!

Mr. Jefferson.[4] You should do it.

Mr. Adams. Oh, no!

Mr. Jefferson. Why will you not? You ought to do it.

Mr. Adams. I will not!

Mr. Jefferson. Why?

Mr. Adams. Reasons enough.

Mr. Jefferson. What can be your reasons?

Mr. Adams. Reason first, you are a Virginian and a Virginian ought to appear at the head of this business. Reason second, I am obnoxious, suspected, and unpopular. You are very much otherwise. Reason third, you can write ten times better than I can.

Mr. Jefferson. Well, if you are decided, I will do the best I can.

Mr. Adams. Very well, when you have drawn it up we will have a meeting.

*(Exeunt Mr. Adams and Mr. Jefferson.)*

### Scene II.—*Washington's Address to his Army. Washington and his army*[5] *in camp on Long Island.*

The time is now near at hand, which must probably determine whether Americans are to be freemen or slaves, whether their houses and farms are to be pillaged and destroyed, and themselves to be consigned to a state of wretchedness from which no human efforts will deliver them. The fate of unborn millions will now depend, under God, on the courage and the conduct of this army. Our cruel and unrelenting enemy leaves us only the choice of a brave resistance or the most abject submission. We have, therefore, to resolve to conquer or to die.

Our own, our country's honor, calls upon us for a vigorous and manly exertion. If we now shamefully fail, we shall become infamous to the whole world. The eyes of all our countrymen are now upon us, and we shall have their blessings and praises if happily we are the instruments of saving them from the tyranny meditated against them. Let us, therefore, animate and encourage each other, and show the whole world that a freeman contending for liberty on his own ground is superior to any slavish mercenary on earth.

---

[4] This dialogue between Adams and Jefferson is taken from Adams's letter to Timothy Pickering.

[5] If this is properly staged it will be very effective. National Guard members will be glad to take part as members of Washington's army, with their tents and uniforms and arms, if there are no school cadets to play this part. The bugler sounds the call to arms. The soldiers fall into line ready for the fight. Just before marching orders are given, Washington delivers the following address, after which the curtain goes down on this scene and the sound of battle is heard in the distance.

Liberty, property, life, and honor are all at stake. Upon your courage and conduct rest the hopes of our bleeding and insulted country. Our wives, children, and parents expect safety from us only; and they have every reason to believe that Heaven will crown with success so just a cause.

The enemy will endeavor to intimidate by show and appearance; but remember that they have been repulsed on various occasions by a few brave Americans. Their cause is bad—their men are conscious of it. If they are opposed with firmness and coolness on their first onset, with our advantage of works and knowledge of the ground, the victory is most assuredly ours.

### Scene III.—Tableau—"The Spirit of '76."

As soon as the sound of battle has died away following the departure of Washington and his army, put on the tableau of "The Spirit of '76." The fifer, the drummer, and the little boy should be good musicians playing patriotic music of the Revolution. Their wounded and ragged comrades are seen in the background.

### Scene IV.—Mr. Jefferson seated at his desk and putting on the finishing touches to his original draft of the Declaration of Independence. Enter Mr. Adams.

Mr. Adams. Good evening, Mr. Jefferson.

Mr. Jefferson. Good evening, Mr. Adams.

Mr. Adams. Well, have you the Declaration finished?

Mr. Jefferson. Mr. Adams, I have done the best I could but I am not very well satisfied with what I have written. I wish you would look it over and make such corrections and criticisms as your judgment deems proper.

Mr. Adams (*studying the Declaration*). Mr. Jefferson, I am delighted with your production. Your statements relative to the inalienable rights of men are unanswerable and to secure these rights, governments *must* be instituted among men, *deriving* their *just powers from* the *consent* of the *governed*. This paragraph concerning negro slavery meets with my approval but I fear it will not meet with the approval of some of the Southern delegates. I congratulate you, Mr. Jefferson, on what you have done. This document will make you immortal.

Mr. Jefferson. Thank you, Mr. Adams, I fear you are too extravagant in your praise of my work.

(*Enter Mr. Franklin and Mr. Sherman.*)

Mr. Franklin. Well, gentlemen, have you completed the draft for the Declaration?

Mr. Adams. Mr. Jefferson has finished it. It is all his work. I have reviewed the paper very hurriedly but in my opinion it is one of the greatest documents ever written by man. Look it over, gentlemen, and let us hear your opinion of it.

Mr. Franklin (*studying the Declaration*). Mr. Jefferson, I congratulate you, sir. Your declaration on the inalienable rights of men is well stated. I agree with you that governments *derive* their *just powers from* the *consent* of the *governed.* I like that paragraph on slavery but I believe that some of the Southern delegates will oppose it. This is a paper of which you should be proud, Mr. Jefferson. I congratulate you, sir. Here, Mr. Sherman, let us have your views on this Declaration.

Mr. Sherman (*studying the Declaration*). You have covered all our grievances in the twenty-seven distinct charges you have made against the present king of Great Britain. We can well afford to submit these facts to a candid world. That paragraph on slavery, Mr. Jefferson, meets with my approval heartily, but I fear some of the Southern delegates will oppose it strongly. We can certainly appeal to the Supreme Judge of the world for the rectitude of our intentions. I believe with you that divine Providence will support us in making this Declaration good. Therefore, I am willing to stand with you in pledging our lives, our fortunes, and our sacred honor to this end. I do not see how I could make any suggestions that would improve it. Mr. Jefferson, I congratulate you on the great work you have done in this paper for our country and for humanity.

Mr. Jefferson. Gentlemen, I thank you all most heartily and sincerely for the compliments you have paid me on this paper, but I am no orator myself, especially for such an occasion as this; therefore, I should like to have Mr. Adams report this Declaration to the Continental Congress, move its adoption for me, and lead in the debates in favor of it.

Mr. Franklin. Gentlemen:—I move that Mr. Adams be requested to report this Declaration to the Congress as desired by Mr. Jefferson.

Mr. Sherman. I second the motion.

Mr. Franklin. Gentlemen, you have heard the motion. As many as favor the same make it known by saying "aye." (*Response of ayes; Mr. Adams is silent.*) The ayes seem to have it, the ayes have it, and the motion is carried for Mr. Adams to so report this Declaration. The committee is adjourned.

CURTAIN

# ACT III.



### *Scene I.—The Continental Congress again in session.*

Mr. Hancock. (*Looking at his watch, as he calls the Congress to order.*) Gentlemen of the Continental Congress:—The time has come to which we adjourned yesterday in order to give the Committee of Five, appointed to draft the Declaration, due time to prepare the same. Are the gentlemen of the Committee present and ready to report?

Mr. Adams. Mr. President and Gentlemen of the Continental Congress:—At the request of Mr. Jefferson and the other members of the Committee, I beg leave to submit the following Declaration for your consideration after it has been read by the secretary of this Congress. Permit me to say here, however, that the credit for the authorship of this paper belongs entirely to Mr. Jefferson. It is his work, which the other members of the Committee are unanimous in approving.

> (*Charles Thomson, secretary of the Congress, reads the Declaration of Independence. This part should be assigned to one who has a good clear voice and is a good public reader. If it is thought best not to read all of the Declaration, its most striking paragraphs should be read. Do not forget to have the famous paragraph on slavery read. If it were omitted the great speech of George Walton would be out of place.*)

John Adams.[6] Mr. President and Gentlemen of the Continental Congress:— Sink or swim, live or die, survive or perish, I give my hand and my heart to this vote in favor of this Declaration of Independence. It is true, indeed, that in the beginning we aimed not at independence. But there's a divinity which shapes our ends. The injustice of England has driven us to arms; and, blinded to her own interest for our good, she has obstinately persisted, till independence is now within our grasp. We have but to reach forth to it, and it is ours. Why, then, should we defer the Declaration?

Is any man so weak as now to hope for a reconciliation with England, which shall leave either safety to the country and its liberties, or safety to his own life and his own honor? Are not you,[7] sir, who sit in that chair, is not he,[8] our venerable colleague near you, are you not both already the proscribed and predestined objects of punishment and of vengeance? Cut off from all hope of royal clemency, what are you, what can you be, while the power of England remains, but outlaws?

[6] This is a part of Webster's "Supposed Speech of John Adams."

[7] John Hancock.

[8] Samuel Adams.

If we postpone independence do we mean to carry on, or to give up the war? Do we mean to submit to the measures of Parliament, Boston Port Bill and all? Do we mean to submit, and consent that we ourselves shall be ground to powder, and our country and its rights trodden down in the dust? I know we do not mean to submit. We never shall submit. Do we intend to violate that most solemn obligation ever entered into by men, that plighting, before God, of our sacred honor to Washington, when, putting him forth to incur the dangers of war, as well as the political hazards of the times, we promised to adhere to him, in every extremity, with our fortunes and our lives? I know there is not a man here who would not rather see a general conflagration sweep over the land, or an earthquake sink it, than one jot or tittle of that plighted faith fall to the ground. For myself, having twelve months ago, in this place, moved you, that George Washington be appointed commander of the forces raised, or to be raised, for defense of American liberty, may my right hand forget her cunning, and my tongue cleave to the roof of my mouth, if I hesitate or waver in the support I give him.

*(At the close of Mr. Adams' speech there is loud clamor for recognition.*
*The president recognizes Edward Rutledge of South Carolina, who*
*speaks against the Declaration.)*

Edward Rutledge.[9]Mr. President and Gentlemen of the Continental Congress:—Let us pause! This step, once taken, cannot be retraced. This resolution, once passed, will cut off all hope of reconciliation. If success attend the arms of England, we shall then be no longer colonies, with charters, and with privileges. These will all be forfeited by this act; and we shall be in the condition of other conquered people—at the mercy of the conquerors. For ourselves, we may be ready to run the hazard; but are we ready to carry the country to that length? Is success so probable as to justify it? Where is the military, where the naval power, by which we are to resist the whole strength of the arm of England? For she will exert that strength to the utmost. Can we rely on the constancy and perseverance of the people?—or will they not act as the people of other countries have acted, and, wearied with a long war, submit in the end, to a worse oppression? While we stand on our old ground, and insist on redress of grievances, we know we are right, and are not answerable for consequences. Nothing, then, can be imputable to us.

*(At the close of Mr. Rutledge's speech there is a clamor for recognition.*
*The president recognizes Roger Sherman of Connecticut.)*

Roger Sherman.[10]Mr. President and Gentlemen of the Continental Congress:—The war must go on. We must fight it through. And if the war must go on, why put off longer the Declaration of Independence? That measure will strengthen us. It will give us character abroad. The nations will then treat with us, which they never can do while we acknowledge ourselves subjects, in arms against our sovereign. Nay, I maintain that England herself will sooner treat for peace with us on the footing of independence, than consent, by repealing her acts, to acknowledge that her whole conduct toward us has been a course of injustice and oppres-

[9] From Webster's "Supposed Speech of Opposition to Independence."
[10] From Webster's "Supposed Speech of John Adams."

sion. Her pride will be less wounded by submitting to the course of things which now predestinates our independence, than by yielding the points in controversy to her rebellious subjects. The former she will regard as the result of fortune; the latter she would feel as her own deep disgrace. Why, then, why, then, sir, do we not as soon as possible change this from a civil to a national war? And since we must fight it through, why not put ourselves in a state to enjoy all the benefits of victory, if we gain the victory?

If we fail, it can be no worse for us. But we shall not fail. The cause will raise up armies; the cause will create navies. The people, the people, if we are true to them will carry us, and will carry themselves, gloriously through this struggle. I care not how fickle other people have been found. I know the people of these colonies, and I know that resistance to British aggression is deep and settled in their hearts, and cannot be eradicated. Every colony, indeed, has expressed its willingness to follow, if we but take the lead. Sir, the Declaration will inspire the people with increased courage. Instead of a long and bloody war for the restoration of privileges, for redress of grievances, for chartered immunities, held under a British king, set before them the glorious object of entire independence, and it will breathe into them anew the breath of life. Read this Declaration at the head of the army; every sword will be drawn from its scabbard, and the solemn vow uttered to maintain it, or to perish on the bed of honor. Publish it from the pulpit, religion will approve it, and the love of religious liberty will cling around it, resolved to stand with it, or fall with it. Send it to the public halls; proclaim it there; let them hear it who heard the first roar of the enemy's cannon; let them see it who saw their brothers and their sons fall on the field of Bunker Hill and in the streets of Lexington and Concord, and the very walls will cry out in its support.

*(At the close of Mr. Sherman's speech there is a loud clamor for recognition. The president recognizes John Dickinson of Pennsylvania.)*

JOHN DICKINSON.[11]Mr. President and Gentlemen of the Continental Congress:—If we now change our object, carry our pretensions farther, and set up for absolute independence, we shall lose the sympathy of mankind. We shall no longer be defending what we possess, but struggling for something which we never did possess, and which we have solemnly and uniformly disclaimed all intention of pursuing, from the very outset of the troubles. Abandoning thus our old ground of resistance only to arbitrary acts of oppression, the nations will believe the whole to have been mere pretense, and they will look on us, not as injured, but as ambitious subjects. I shudder before this responsibility. It will be upon us, it will be upon us, if, relinquishing the ground we have stood upon so long, and stood so safely, we now proclaim independence, and carry on the war for that object, while these cities burn, these pleasant fields whiten and bleach with the bones of their owners, and these streams run blood. It will be upon us, it will be upon us, if failing to maintain this unseasonable and ill-judged Declaration, a sterner despotism, maintained by military power, shall be established over our posterity, when we ourselves, given up by an exhausted, a harassed, a misled people, shall have expiated our rashness and atoned for our presumption on the scaffold.

[11] From Webster's "Supposed Speech of Opposition to Independence."

## BENJAMIN FRANKLIN

*(At the close of Mr. Dickinson's speech there is a loud clamor for recognition. The president recognizes Benjamin Franklin of Pennsylvania.)*

BENJAMIN FRANKLIN.[12]Mr. President and Gentlemen of the Continental Congress:—I know the uncertainty of human affairs, but I see, I see clearly, through this day's business. You and I, indeed, may rue it. We may not live to the time when this Declaration shall be made good. We may die; die colonists; die slaves; die, it may be ignominiously and on the scaffold. Be it so. Be it so. If it be the pleasure of Heaven that my country shall require the poor offering of my life, the victim shall be ready, at the appointed hour of sacrifice, come when that hour may.

---

[12] From Webster's "Supposed Speech of John Adams."

But while I do live, let me have a country, or at least the hope of a country, and that a free country.

But whatever may be our fate, be assured, be assured that this Declaration will stand. It may cost treasure, and it may cost blood; but it will stand, and it will richly compensate for both. Through the thick gloom of the present, I see the brightness of the future as the sun in heaven. We shall make this a glorious, an immortal day. When we are in our graves, our children will honor it. They will celebrate it with thanksgiving, with festivity, with bonfires, and illuminations. On its annual return they will shed tears, copious, gushing tears, not of subjection and slavery, not of agony and distress, but of exultation, of gratitude, and of joy. Sir, before God, I believe the hour has come. My whole heart is in it. All that I have, and all that I am, and all that I hope in this life, I am now ready here to stake upon it; and I leave off as Mr. Adams of Massachusetts began, that, sink or swim, live or die, survive or perish, I am for the Declaration. It is my living sentiment, and by the blessing of God it shall be my dying sentiment, independence *now, and* INDE-PENDENCE FOREVER!

*(There is a loud clamor for recognition, and the president recognizes*
*George Walton of Georgia.)*

GEORGE WALTON.[13]Mr. President and Gentlemen of the Continental Congress:—I am for this Declaration if the paragraph on slavery is struck out. But I will oppose it to the end if that paragraph is permitted to remain a part of it. There is not one good reason for introducing the slavery question at this time. The relations between individual master and slave have no place here in the greater and graver matter of differences between the British Government and the American Colonies. But since the issue is thrust upon us, I propose to meet it squarely and fearlessly.

Mr. President and gentlemen, you cannot make equal what God Almighty has made unequal. Can the Ethiopian change his skin or the leopard his spots? The Bible commands in the most emphatic language that servants obey in all things their masters. Liberty loving Greece had her slaves. Shall liberty loving America have less? Strike out that obnoxious paragraph and every delegate from the Southern colonies will fall in line for the Declaration of Independence, but if you make that paragraph a part of the Declaration many delegates from the South will withdraw from this convention, and then you will fight your own battles.

This paragraph on slavery is founded upon ideas fundamentally wrong. These ideas rest upon the assumption of the equality of the races. This is an error. It is a sandy foundation and a government founded upon it will fall when the storms come and the winds blow.

Let us found our new government upon the great truth that the negro is not the equal of the white man, that slavery—subordination to the superior race—is his natural and normal condition. This truth has been slow in the process of its development, like all other great truths in the various departments of science.

---

[13] Adapted from the "Corner Stone" speech of Alexander H. Stephens, and arranged by William R. Hood, Bureau of Education, Washington, D. C.

Many governments have been founded upon the principle of the subordination and serfdom of certain classes of the *same* race; such were and are in violation of the laws of nature. With us, *all* the *white* race, however high or low, rich or poor, are equal in the eye of the law. Not so with the negro; subordination is his place. He, by nature or by the curse of Canaan, is fitted for that condition which he now occupies in our system. The architect, in the construction of a building, lays the foundation with proper material—the granite; then comes the brick or the marble. The substratum of our society is made of the material fitted by nature for it, and by experience we know that it is best not only for the superior race, but for the inferior race, that it should be so. It is, indeed, in conformity with the laws of the Creator. It is not for us to inquire into the wisdom of His plans, or to question them. For His own good purposes He has made one race to differ from another, as He has made "one star to differ from another star in glory."

Therefore, I declare again that you cannot make equal what God Almighty has made unequal. He has made the negro and the white man unequal. You cannot make them equal. And I move that the paragraph on slavery be struck out. I have measured my words, gentlemen. The responsibility is yours.

*(At the close of Mr. Walton's speech there is a loud clamor for recognition, and the chair recognizes Samuel Adams.)*

Samuel Adams. Mr. President and Gentlemen:—While I have no personal objections against this paragraph on slavery—for personally I favor it—yet from the standpoint of the general welfare of the colonies, I deem it unwise at this time to take any action either for or against the question of slavery. Therefore I second the motion of Mr. Walton to strike out the paragraph on slavery.

Mr. Hancock. Gentlemen of the Continental Congress:—It has been duly moved and seconded that the paragraph in this Declaration on slavery be struck out. You have heard the motion, are there any remarks?

William Hooper. Mr. President, before voting on this motion, I wish to have the paragraph on slavery read again.

*(This request is seconded by many of the delegates.)*

Mr. Hancock. The secretary will read the paragraph on slavery again.

*(The secretary reads the paragraph on slavery as follows:)*

He has waged cruel war against human nature itself, violating its most sacred rights of life and liberty in the persons of a distant people who never offended him, captivating and carrying them into slavery in another hemisphere, or to incur miserable death in their transportation thither. This piratical warfare, the opprobrium of infidel powers, is the warfare of the Christian king of Great Britain. Determined to keep open a market where men should be bought and sold, he has prostituted his negative for suppressing every legislative attempt to prohibit or to restrain this execrable commerce. And that this assemblage of horrors might want no fact of distinguished dye, he is now exciting those very people to rise in arms among us and to purchase that liberty of which he has deprived them by murdering the people upon whom he obtruded them: thus paying off, former crimes committed against the *liberties* of one people, with crimes which he urges them to commit against the *lives* of another.

(*After the reading of this paragraph the delegates call for a vote on Mr. Walton's motion.*)

Mr. Hancock. Gentlemen of the Congress, a vote is called for on Mr. Walton's motion to strike out the paragraph on slavery. As many as are in favor of this motion make it known by saying "aye" (*a strong aye vote*); as many as are opposed to the motion make it known by responding "no" (*a light vote of noes*). The ayes seem to have it, the ayes have it, and the paragraph on slavery is struck out. Gentlemen, what is your further pleasure?

(*A loud clamor for recognition, the chair recognizing Joseph Hewes of North Carolina.*)

Joseph Hewes.[14] Mr. President and Gentlemen of the Continental Congress:— No man thinks more highly than I do of the patriotism, as well as the abilities, of the very worthy gentlemen who have opposed this Declaration in these debates. But different men often see the same subject in different lights; and, therefore, I hope it will not be thought disrespectful to those gentlemen, if, entertaining, as I do, opinions of a character very opposite to theirs, I shall speak forth my sentiments freely and without reserve. This is no time for ceremony. The question before the house is one of awful moment to this country. For my own part, I consider it as nothing less than a question of freedom or slavery; and in proportion to the magnitude of the subject ought to be the freedom of debate. It is only in this way that we can hope to arrive at truth, and fulfill the great responsibility which we hold to God and our country. Should I keep back my opinions at such a time, through fear of giving offense, I should consider myself as guilty of treason toward my country, and of an act of disloyalty toward the Majesty of Heaven, which I revere above all earthly kings.

Mr. President, it is natural for man to indulge in the illusions of hope. We are apt to shut our eyes against a painful truth, and listen to the song of that siren, till she transforms us into beasts. Is this the part of wise men, engaged in a great and arduous struggle for liberty? Are we disposed to be of the number of those, who, having eyes, see not, and having ears, hear not, the things which so nearly concern their temporal salvation? For my part, whatever anguish of spirit it may cost, I am willing to know the truth; to know the worst, and to provide for it.

I have but one lamp by which my feet are guided; and that is the lamp of experience. I know of no way of judging of the future but by the past. And judging by the past, I wish to know what there has been in the conduct of the British ministry for the last ten years, to justify those hopes with which gentlemen have been pleased to solace themselves and the house? Is it that insidious smile with which our petition has been lately received? Trust it not, sir; it will prove a snare to your feet. Suffer not yourselves to be betrayed with a kiss. Ask yourselves how this gracious reception of our petition comports with those warlike preparations which cover our waters and darken our land. Are fleets and armies necessary to a work of

[14] From Wirt's "Supposed Speech of Patrick Henry."

love and reconciliation? Have we shown ourselves so unwilling to be reconciled, that force must be called in to win back our love? Let us not deceive ourselves, sir. These are the implements of war and subjugation; the last arguments to which kings resort. I ask gentlemen, sir, what means this martial array, if its purpose be not to force us to submission? Can gentlemen assign any other possible motive for it? Has Great Britain any enemy, in this quarter of the world, that calls for all this accumulation of navies and armies? No, sir, she has none. They are meant for us; they can be meant for no other. They are sent over to bind and rivet upon us those chains, which the British ministry have been so long forging. And what have we to oppose to them? Shall we try argument? Sir, we have been trying that for the last ten years. Have we anything new to offer upon the subject? Nothing! We have held the subject up in every light of which it is capable; but it has been all in vain. Shall we resort to entreaty and humble supplication? What terms shall we find, which have not been already exhausted? Let us not. I beseech you, sir, deceive ourselves longer.

*(A loud clamor for recognition. The chair recognizes Robert Morris of Pennsylvania.)*

ROBERT MORRIS.[15]Mr. President and Gentlemen of the Continental Congress:—I am opposed to war first, last, and all the time. It is a relic of barbarism. I believe in the gospel of peace on earth, good will toward men. It would be better to settle our differences with England even by flipping a coin than by fighting and killing one another. Let us hearken unto the voice of God as it comes ringing down the centuries from Mount Sinai, "Thou shalt not kill." Shall this new government start out as the Cain among the nations of earth with the blood of our brethren upon our hands? God forbid that we make ourselves so foolish and so reckless as this! The history of trial by battle is the history of folly and wickedness. As we revert to those early periods in the history of the human race in which it prevailed, our minds are shocked at the barbarism which we behold; we are horror stricken at the awful subjection of justice to brute force.

Who told you, fond man! to regard that as glory when performed by a nation, which is condemned as a crime and a barbarism, when committed by an individual? In what vain conceit of wisdom and virtue do you find this degrading morality? Where is it declared that God, who is no respecter of persons, is a respecter of multitudes? Whence do you draw these partial laws of a powerful and impartial God? Man is immortal; but states are mortal. Man has a higher destiny than states. Shall states be less amenable to the great moral laws of God than man? Each individual is an atom of the mass. Must not the mass be like individuals of which it is composed? Shall the mass do what the individual may not do? No! A thousand times *NO!* The same laws which govern individuals govern masses, as the same laws in nature prevail over large and small things, controlling the fall of an apple and the orbits of the planets.

And who is this god of battles that some of you men believe in with so much

---

[15] Robert Morris later signed the Declaration of Independence and through his influence the American Revolution was financed. This speech is adapted from Sumner's "True Grandeur of Nations" and other sources.

faith? It is Mars—man-slaying, blood-polluted, city-smiting, Mars! Him we cannot adore. It is not he who causes the sun to shine on the just and the unjust. It is not he who tempers the wind to the shorn lamb. It is not he who distills the oil of gladness in every upright heart. It is not he who fills the fountain of mercy and goodness. He is not the God of love and justice. The god of battles is not the God of Christians; to him can ascend no prayer of Christian thanksgiving; for him no words of worship in Christian temples, no swelling anthem to peal the note of praise.

Let us cease, then, to look for a lamp to our feet in the feeble tapers that glimmer in the sepulchers of the past. Rather let us hail those ever-burning lights above in whose beams is the brightness of the noon-day. As the cedars of Lebanon are higher than the grass of the valley, as the heavens are higher than the earth, as man is higher than the beasts of the field, as the angels are higher than man, as he that ruleth his spirit is higher than he that taketh a city; so are the virtues and glories and victories of peace higher than the virtues and victories of war.

To this great work of world-wide peace let me summon you. Believe that you can do it, and you can do it. Blessed are the peace-makers for they are the children of God.

*(Loud clamor for recognition, the chair recognizing Patrick Henry of Virginia.)*

PATRICK HENRY.[16]Mr. President and Gentlemen of the Continental Congress:—We have done everything that could be done, to avert the storm which is now coming on. We have petitioned; we have remonstrated; we have supplicated; we have prostrated ourselves before the throne, and have implored its interposition to arrest the tyrannical hands of the ministry and Parliament. Our petitions have been slighted; our remonstrances have produced additional violence and insult; our supplications have been disregarded; and we have been spurned, with contempt, from the foot of the throne! In vain, after these things, may we indulge the fond hope of peace and reconciliation. There is no longer any room for hope. If we wish to be free—if we mean to preserve inviolate those inestimable privileges for which we have been so long contending—if we mean not basely to abandon the noble struggle in which we have been so long engaged, and which we have pledged ourselves never to abandon, until the glorious object of our contest shall be obtained—we must fight! I repeat it, sir, we must fight! An appeal to arms and to the God of Hosts is all that is left us.

They tell us, sir, that we are weak; unable to cope with so formidable an adversary. But when shall we be stronger? Will it be the next week, or the next year? Will it be when we are totally disarmed, and when a British guard shall be stationed in every house? Shall we gather strength by irresolution and inaction? Shall we acquire the means of effectual resistance, by lying supinely on our backs and hugging the delusive phantom of hope, until our enemies shall have bound us hand and foot? Sir, we are not weak, if we make proper use of those means which the God of nature hath placed in our power. Three millions of people, armed in the holy cause of liberty, and in such a country as that which we possess, are invinci-

---

[16] From Wirt's "Supposed Speech of Patrick Henry."

ble by any force which our enemy can send against us. Besides, sir, we shall not fight our battles alone. There is a just God who presides over the destinies of nations, and who will raise up friends to fight our battles for us. The battle, sir, is not to the strong alone; it is to the vigilant, the active, the brave. Besides, sir, we have no election. If we were base enough to desire it, it is now too late to retire from the contest. There is no retreat, but in submission and slavery! Our chains are forged. Their clanking may be heard on the plains of Boston. The war is inevitable—and let it come! I repeat it, sir, let it come.

It is in vain, sir, to extenuate the matter. Gentlemen may cry, Peace, peace—but there is no peace. The war is actually begun! The next gale, that sweeps from the north, will bring to our ears the clash of resounding arms! Our brethren are already in the field! Why stand we here idle? What is it that gentlemen wish? What would they have? Is life so dear, or peace so sweet, as to be purchased at the price of chains and slavery? Forbid it, Almighty God! I know not what course others may take; but as for me, give me liberty or give me death!

*(At the close of Mr. Henry's speech there are loud calls for a vote upon the question. President Hancock orders the secretary to call the roll of colonies in geographic order beginning with New Hampshire.)*

SECRETARY THOMSON. New Hampshire!

JOSIAH BARTLETT. Mr. President and Gentlemen:—New Hampshire is represented in the Congress by three delegates. Her people have appealed to us and have instructed us to work for and vote for Independence. I believe everybody knows more than any body. I consider it a signal honor, sir, and it is the happiest hour of my life, to lead in this roll call in favor of this Declaration. New Hampshire votes *aye.*

*(Shouts of "Three cheers for New Hampshire.")*

SECRETARY THOMSON. Massachusetts!

SAMUEL ADAMS. Mr. President:—The king of England has set a price upon your head and mine. If this Declaration is not made good by the people of these colonies you and I will be shot, hanged by the neck till dead, or burned at the stake as traitors. If we fail, my only regret will be that I have but one life to give for my country. But with faith in the people and in God to carry our cause through to a glorious victory, the delegates from Massachusetts stand as one man for Independence. Massachusetts, therefore, votes *aye.*

*(Shouts of "Three cheers for Massachusetts, and long live Samuel Adams and John Hancock. Down with the tyrant king of England!")*

SECRETARY THOMSON. Rhode Island!

STEPHEN HOPKINS. Mr. President:—Rhode Island is a small colony. She is represented in this Congress by only two delegates. But all that we are and all we hope to be we are ready here and now to give for Independence. Rhode Island votes *aye.*

*(Shouts of "Three cheers for brave Rhode Island, Stephen Hopkins, and*

*William Ellery.")*

Secretary Thomson. Connecticut!

Roger Sherman. Mr. President and Gentlemen:—I have already addressed you at some length in favor of this Declaration. It becomes my happy duty now to cast the unanimous vote of the four delegates from Connecticut for independence. Connecticut votes *aye.*

*(Shouts of "Long live Roger Sherman! Three cheers for Connecticut.")*

*Secretary Thomson.* New York!

William Floyd. Mr. President and Gentlemen:—The instructions against independence for the delegates from New York have never been recalled. We, therefore, request the privilege to refrain from voting on this question. We regret the situation, gentlemen!

President Hancock. New York is excused from voting on this question.

Secretary Thomson. New Jersey!

Richard Stockton. Mr. President and Gentlemen:—I am happy to say that New Jersey has given her five delegates in this Congress instructions to vote for independence. New Jersey, therefore, votes *aye.*

*(Shouts of "Three cheers for New Jersey.")*

Secretary Thomson. Pennsylvania!

Benjamin Franklin. Mr. President and Gentlemen:—From the beginning of this Congress the delegates from Pennsylvania have labored under instructions against independence. But during the past three months the friends of independence in this commonwealth have worked in season and out of season to have these instructions canceled and permission given us to vote for independence. At a mass meeting in Philadelphia on June 18, presided over by that distinguished and influential radical, Colonel Daniel Roberdeau, and attended by over 7,000 citizens from all sections of the state, a public sentiment was created and started that resulted in the overthrow of the old government of the aristocrats of the old Assembly and then established a new government of the people under the authority of the Conference of Committees which has given the delegates from Pennsylvania instructions to vote for independence. Two of our delegates, John Dickinson and Robert Morris, have retired from this Congress considering such instructions a recall of their membership in this body. Two other delegates from Pennsylvania, Charles Humphreys and William Williams, question the authority of the Conference of Committees and hold that the instructions of the old defunct Assembly are still binding upon them. They vote against independence. But James Wilson who has been opposed to Independence bows to the will of the people and joins John Morton and myself in voting for Independence. Under the rule of this Congress made in its beginning session that a majority of the delegates from each colony, present and voting determines its vote upon such a question as this, Pennsylvania casts two votes against independence and three votes for independence and therefore votes *aye.*

*(Shouts of "Three cheers for Pennsylvania! Long live Benjamin Franklin, John Morton, and James Wilson!")*

*(Immediately following the applause for Franklin, Caesar Rodney, a delegate from Delaware, makes his appearance just in time to vote. He has come eighty miles on horseback and has not had time to change his boots and spurs and still carries a riding whip. He is given a great ovation.)*

SECRETARY THOMSON. Delaware!

THOMAS McKEAN. Mr. President and Gentlemen:—Until this moment the vote for Delaware has been in doubt. George Read, my colleague, will vote against independence. But thank God the timely arrival of Caesar Rodney who joins me in voting for independence, places Delaware on the right side of this question. To make sure of this I sent an express rider at my own expense to Dover, Delaware, for Mr. Rodney. He has come eighty miles on horseback at post-haste. He has not had time to change his riding attire, but he is here in time to join me in voting for independence. Posterity will erect a monument in his honor[17] as they will to that other famous revolutionary rider—Paul Revere. Mr. President, under the rule as stated by Mr. Franklin governing the votes of colonies in this Congress, Delaware votes *aye*.

*(Shouts of "Hurrah for Delaware! Long live Thomas McKean and Caesar Rodney!")*

SECRETARY THOMSON. Maryland!

SAMUEL CHASE. Mr. President and Gentlemen:—Maryland has passed through a similar struggle to that in Pennsylvania as described by Mr. Franklin. An appeal has been made to every county committee and one after another they have directed their representatives in the state convention to vote for new instructions to the delegates in this Congress. At last the old instructions against independence have been canceled and new instructions given us in an unanimous resolve to vote for independence. See the glorious effect of county instructions! Our people have fire if not smothered. And, therefore, Maryland votes *aye*.

*(Shouts of "Three cheers for Maryland and Samuel Chase!")*

SECRETARY THOMSON. Virginia!

BENJAMIN HARRISON. Mr. President and Gentlemen:—Virginia is here with a solid delegation for independence. Our battle cry has been so well stated by Mr. Henry that we need but to repeat it now—Liberty or Death! Virginia votes *aye*.

*(Shouts of "Three cheers for Virginia! Long live Richard Henry Lee, Benjamin Harrison, Thomas Jefferson and Patrick Henry!")*

SECRETARY THOMSON. North Carolina!

JOSEPH HEWES. Mr. President and Gentlemen:—We have had a hard struggle in North Carolina between aristocracy on one hand and democracy on the other. But at last the people have won and North Carolina votes *aye*.

[17] A monument was recently erected at Dover in his honor.

*(Shouts of "Three cheers for North Carolina!")*

### THE CONTINENTAL CONGRESS

*From the painting by Trumbull*

SECRETARY THOMSON. South Carolina!

EDWARD RUTLEDGE. Mr. President and Gentlemen:—When Richard Henry Lee's resolution declaring for independence was first introduced I was opposed to its adoption *at that time*. I feared that the people of my colony were not then ready for it. I thought also that for the general welfare of all the colonies it was then too early to declare for independence. The contest in South Carolina for independence has been as bitter among her own people as it has been in any of the other colonies. But opinions alter and conditions change with the passing of time. Therefore, South Carolina now has a solid delegation here ready to walk through the fiery furnace of war, though it be seventy times heated, to make this Declaration good. South Carolina votes *aye*.

*(Shouts of "Three cheers for South Carolina and Edward Rutledge!")*

SECRETARY THOMSON. Georgia!

LYMAN HALL. Mr. President and Gentlemen:—Georgia is here with three delegates who stand as one man for independence. Though last on the roll of states on this question she will be among the first in her efforts for American independence. Georgia votes *aye*.

*(Shouts of "Three cheers for Georgia!")*

PRESIDENT HANCOCK. Gentlemen of the Continental Congress:—Twelve of the thirteen colonies having voted for the Declaration of Independence, and with no colony going on record against it, I consider our action unanimous for I am confident that the New York Assembly[18] will give her delegation instructions to sign this document in the near future.

JOHN ADAMS. Mr. President, I move that this Congress do now adjourn.

BENJAMIN FRANKLIN. Mr. President, I second the motion.

PRESIDENT HANCOCK. Gentlemen of the Continental Congress, it has been moved by Mr. Adams of Massachusetts and seconded by Mr. Franklin of Pennsylvania that we do now adjourn. As many as favor this motion make known by saying *aye*.

*(Unanimous response of ayes.)*

The motion to adjourn has been carried unanimously and this Congress is therefore adjourned.

## SCENE II.—*The Spirit of 76.*

Here repeat the Tableau of the Spirit of Seventy-six.

---

[18] On July 9, 1776, New York instructed her delegates to sign.

# ACT IV.



*SCENE I.—Washington's Resignation. (A special session of the Continental Congress to receive the Resignation of Washington.)*

PRESIDENT HANCOCK. Gentlemen of the Continental Congress:—Eight years ago we made General George Washington Commander-in-Chief of the armies raised and to be raised for American Independence. Through seven long years of war, against overwhelming odds, in which brave men did brave deeds, the rich man gave his wealth and the poor man gave his life, baptizing their country's soil with their own blood from Bunker Hill to Yorktown, the brave soldiers under General Washington fought on until an army of veteran soldiers surrendered to a band of insurgent husbandmen. The American nation has been born. Its independence has been recognized by Great Britain and the civilized world. Peace has come! And General Washington desires to surrender his commission to the Congress that elected him to this position. He is in waiting to do this. I therefore appoint John Adams of Massachusetts, Benjamin Franklin of Pennsylvania, Roger Sherman of Connecticut, Samuel Chase of Maryland, Patrick Henry of Virginia, Edward Rutledge of South Carolina, and Lyman Hall of Georgia, as an honorary committee to escort General Washington before this Congress, to receive his resignation.

*(General Washington is escorted before Congress and makes the following address:)*

*Mr. President:*—The great events on which my resignation depended, having at length taken place, I have now the honor of offering my sincere congratulations to Congress, and of presenting myself before them to surrender into their hands the trust committed to me, and to claim the indulgence of retiring from the service of my country.

Happy in the confirmation of our independence and sovereignty, and pleased with the opportunity afforded the United States of becoming a respectable nation, I resign, with satisfaction, the appointment I accepted with diffidence; a diffidence in my abilities to accomplish so arduous a task, which, however, was superseded by a confidence in the rectitude of our cause, the support of the Supreme Power of the Union, and the patronage of Heaven.

The successful termination of the war has verified the most sanguine expectations; and my gratitude for the interposition of Providence, and the assistance I have received from my countrymen, increases with every review of the momentous contest.

While I repeat my obligations to the army in general, I should do injustice to my own feelings, not to acknowledge, in this place, the peculiar services and distinguished merits of the persons who have been attached to my person during the war. It was impossible the choice of confidential officers to compose my family could have been more fortunate. Permit me sir, to recommend in particular those who have continued in the service to the present moment as worthy of the favorable notice and patronage of Congress.

I consider it as an indispensable duty to close this last solemn act of my official life, by commending the interests of our dearest country to the protection of Almighty God, and those who have the superintendence of them to his holy keeping.

Having now finished the work assigned me, I retire from the great theater of action; and, bidding an affectionate farewell to this august body, under whose orders I have long acted, I here offer my commission, and take my leave of all the employments of public life.

*(The Continental Congress, standing and shouting in concert, "Long live General George Washington! First in war! First in peace! And First in the hearts of his countrymen!")*

CURTAIN

# AMERICAN PATRIOTISM

GEORGE WASHINGTON

# WHAT IS PATRIOTISM

## JASPER L. MCBRIEN

Johnson defines a patriot as one whose ruling passion is the love of his country, and patriotism as love and zeal for one's country. Curtis tells us that Lowell's pursuit was literature, but patriotism was his passion. "His love of country was that of a lover for his mistress. He resented the least imputation upon the ideal America, and nothing was finer than his instinctive scorn for the pinchbeck patriotism which brags and boasts and swaggers, insisting that bigness is greatness and vulgarity simplicity, and the will of a majority the moral law."

While some of us cannot make Lowell's pursuit our pursuit, we all can and should make his passion our passion. Let us all, the native born as well as the naturalized, say, deep down in our hearts with a patriotism and a courage that will back it up and make it good, "Our Country—right or wrong; if she is wrong we will set her right; if she is right we will keep her right; and so let us trust in God and believe she is right."

Times like these demand men. Let American boys be taught in the home and in the school and by the example of their fathers to be men among men.

> "Men whom the lust of office will not kill,
> Men whom the spoils of office cannot buy,
> Men who possess opinions and a will,
> Men who have honor and will not lie;
> Men who can stand before the demagogue
> And down his treacherous flattering without winking,
> Tall men, sun crowned, who live above the fog
> In public duty and in private thinking!"[19]

Times like these demand women! Let American girls be taught in the home and in the school and by the example of their mothers to be women among women.

> "Be women! on to duty!
> Raise the world from all that's low;
> Place high in the social heaven
> Virtue's fair and radiant bow;
> Lend thy influence to each effort
> That shall raise our nature human;
> Be not fashion's gilded ladies,—

[19] From the poem entitled "Wanted," by J. G. Holland.

Be brave, whole-souled, true women!"[20]

To help to make such men and women of all American boys and girls—Americans in *deeds* as well as in *words*—Americans, who knowing their rights, dare maintain them *"without compromise and at any cost"*—this is the purpose of the following selections.

Jasper L. McBrien.

---

[20] Edward Brooks.

# AMERICA FOR ME[21]

## HENRY VAN DYKE

'Tis fine to see the Old World, and travel up and down
Among the famous palaces and cities of renown,
To admire the crumbly castles and the statues of the kings—
But now I think I've had enough of antiquated things.

*So it's home again, and home again, America for me!*
*My heart is turning home again, and there I long to be,*
*In the land of youth and freedom beyond the ocean bars,*
*Where the air is full of sunlight and the flag is full of stars.*

Oh! London is a man's town, there's power in the air;
And Paris is a woman's town, with flowers in her hair;
And it's sweet to dream in Venice, and it's great to study Rome;
But when it comes to living, there is no place like home.

I like the German fir-woods, in green battalions drilled;
I like the gardens of Versailles with flashing fountains filled;
But, oh, to take your hand, my dear, and ramble for a day
In the friendly western woodland where Nature has her way!

I know that Europe's wonderful, yet something seems to lack:
The Past is too much with her, and the people looking back.
But the glory of the Present is to make the Future free—
We love our land for what she is and what she is to be.

*Oh, it's home again, and home again, America for me!*
*I want a ship that's westward bound to plough the rolling sea,*
*To the blessed Land of Room Enough beyond the ocean bars,*
*Where the air is full of sunlight and the flag is full of stars.*

Henry van Dyke

---

[21] From "White Bees and Other Poems," by Henry van Dyke, copyright, 1909, by Charles Scribner's Sons. By permission of Charles Scribner's Sons, publishers.

# AMERICA FIRST

## WOODROW WILSON

The following address was delivered by President Wilson at the celebration of the twenty-fifth anniversary of the Daughters of the American Revolution, Washington, D. C., October 11th, 1915. It is given here by special permission of the president.

Madam President and Ladies and Gentlemen:—Again it is my very great privilege to welcome you to the city of Washington and to the hospitalities of the Capital. May I admit a point of ignorance? I was surprised to learn that this association is so young, and that an association so young should devote itself wholly to memory I cannot believe. For to me the duties to which you are consecrated are more than the duties and the pride of memory.

There is a very great thrill to be had from the memories of the American Revolution, but the American Revolution was a beginning, not a consummation, and the duty laid upon us by that beginning is the duty of bringing the things then begun to a noble triumph of completion. For it seems to me that the peculiarity of patriotism in America is that it is not a mere sentiment. It is an active principle of conduct. It is something that was born into the world, not to please it but to regenerate it. It is something that was born into the world to replace systems that had preceded it and to bring men out upon a new plane of privilege. The glory of the men whose memories you honor and perpetuate is that they saw this vision, and it was a vision of the future. It was a vision of great days to come when a little handful of three million people upon the borders of a single sea should have become a great multitude of free men and women spreading across a great continent, dominating the shores of two oceans, and sending West as well as East the influences of individual freedom. These things were consciously in their minds as they framed the great Government which was born out of the American Revolution; and every time we gather to perpetuate their memories it is incumbent upon us that we should be worthy of recalling them and that we should endeavor by every means in our power to emulate their example.

The American Revolution was the birth of a nation; it was the creation of a great free republic based upon traditions of personal liberty which theretofore had been confined to a single little island, but which it was purposed should spread to all mankind. And the singular fascination of American history is that it has been a process of constant re-creation, of making over again in each generation the thing which was conceived at first. You know how peculiarly necessary that has been in our case, because America has not grown by the mere multiplication of the original stock. It is easy to preserve tradition with continuity of blood; it is easy in a single family to remember the origins of the race and the purposes of its organization; but it is not so easy when that race is constantly being renewed and augmented from other sources, from stocks that did not carry or originate the same principles.

So from generation to generation strangers have had to be indoctrinated with the principles of the American family, and the wonder and the beauty of it all has been that the infection has been so generously easy. For the principles of liberty are united with the principles of hope. Every individual, as well as every nation, wishes to realize the best thing that is in him, the best thing that can be conceived out of the materials of which his spirit is constructed. It has happened in a way that fascinates the imagination that we have not only been augmented by additions from outside, but that we have been greatly stimulated by those additions. Living in the easy prosperity of a free people, knowing that the sun had always been free to shine upon us and prosper our undertakings, we did not realize how hard the task of liberty is and how rare the privilege of liberty is; but men were drawn out of every climate and out of every race because of an irresistible attraction of their spirits to the American ideal. They thought of America as lifting, like that great statue in the harbor of New York, a torch to light the pathway of men to the things that they desire, and men of all sorts and conditions struggled toward that light and came to our shores with an eager desire to realize it, and a hunger for it such as some of us no longer felt, for we were as if satiated and satisfied and were indulging ourselves after a fashion that did not belong to the ascetic devotion of the early devotees of those great principles. Strangers came to remind us of what we had promised ourselves and through ourselves had promised mankind. All men came to us and said, "Where is the bread of life with which you promised to feed us, and have you partaken of it yourselves?" For my part, I believe that the constant renewal of this people out of foreign stocks has been a constant source of reminder to this people of what the inducement was that was offered to men who would come and be of our number.

Now we have come to a time of special stress and test. There never was time when we needed more clearly to conserve the principles of our own patriotism than this present time. The rest of the world from which our polities were drawn seems for the time in the crucible and no man can predict what will come out of that crucible. We stand apart, unembroiled, conscious of our own principles, conscious of what we hope and purpose, so far as our powers permit, for the world at large, and it is necessary that we should consolidate the American principle. Every political action, every social action, should have for its object in America at this time to challenge the spirit of America; to ask that every man and woman who thinks first of America should rally to the standards of our life. There have been some among us who have not thought first of America, who have thought to use the might of America in some matter not of America's origination. They have forgotten that the first duty of a nation is to express its own individual principles in the action of the family of nations and not to seek to aid and abet any rival or contrary ideal. Neutrality is a negative word. It is a word that does not express what America ought to feel. America has a heart and that heart throbs with all sorts of intense sympathies, but America has schooled its heart to love the things that America believes in and it ought to devote itself only to the things that America believes in; and, believing that America stands apart in its ideals, it ought not to allow itself to be drawn, so far as its heart is concerned, into anybody's quarrel. Not because it does not understand the quarrel, not because it does not in its head assess the merits of the controversy, but because America has promised the world to stand apart and maintain certain principles of action which are grounded in law and in justice. We are not trying to keep out of trouble; we are trying to preserve the foundations upon which peace can be rebuilt. Peace can be rebuilt only upon the ancient and accepted principles of international law, only upon those things which remind nations of their duties to each other, and, deeper than that, of their duties to mankind and to humanity.

America has a great cause which is not confined to the American continent. It is the cause of humanity itself. I do not mean in anything that I say even to imply a judgment upon any nation or upon any policy, for my object here this afternoon is not to sit in judgment upon anybody but ourselves and to challenge you to assist all of us who are trying to make America more than ever conscious of her own principles and her own duty. I look forward to the necessity in every political agitation in the years which are immediately at hand of calling upon every man to declare himself, where he stands. Is it America first, or is it not?

We ought to be very careful about some of the impressions that we are forming just now. There is too general an impression, I fear, that very large numbers of our fellow citizens born in other lands have not entertained with sufficient intensity and affection the American ideal. But the number of such is, I am sure, not large. Those who would seek to represent them are very vocal, but they are not very influential. Some of the best stuff of America has come out of foreign lands, and some of the best stuff in America is in the men who are naturalized citizens of the United States. I would not be afraid upon the test of "America first" to take a census of all the foreign-born citizens of the United States, for I know that the vast majority of them came here because they believed in America; and their belief in America has made them better citizens than some people who were born in America. They can say that they have bought this privilege with a great price. They have left their homes, they have left their kindred, they have broken all the nearest and dearest ties of human life in order to come to a new land, take a new rootage, begin a new life, and so by self-sacrifice express their confidence in a new principle; whereas, it cost us none of these things. We were born into this privilege; we were rocked and cradled in it; we did nothing to create it; and it is, therefore, the greater duty on our part to do a great deal to enhance it and preserve it. I am not deceived as to the balance of opinion among the foreign-born citizens of the United States, but I am in a hurry for an opportunity to have a line-up and let the men who are thinking first of other countries stand on one side and all those that are for America first, last, and all the time on the other side.

Now, you can do a great deal in this direction. When I was a college officer. I used to be very much opposed to hazing; not because hazing is not wholesome, but because sophomores are poor judges. I remember a very dear friend of mine, a professor of ethics on the other side of the water, was asked if he thought it was ever justifiable to tell a lie. He said Yes, he thought it was sometimes justifiable to lie; "but," he said, "it is so difficult to judge of the justification that I usually tell the truth." I think that ought to be the motto of the sophomore. There are freshmen who need to be hazed, but the need is to be judged by such nice tests that a sophomore is hardly old enough to determine them. But the world can determine them. We are not freshmen at college, but we are constantly hazed. I would a great deal rather be obliged to draw pepper up my nose than to observe the hostile glances of my neighbors. I would a great deal rather be beaten than ostracized. I would a great deal rather endure any sort of physical hardship if I might have the affection of my fellow men. We constantly discipline our fellow citizens by having an opinion about them. That is the sort of discipline we ought now to administer to everybody who is not to the very core of his heart an American. Just have an opinion about him and let him experience the atmospheric effects of that opinion! And I know of no body of persons comparable to a body of ladies for creating an atmosphere of opinion! I have myself in part yielded to the influences of that atmosphere, though it took me a long time to determine how I was going to vote in New Jersey.

So it has seemed to me that my privilege this afternoon was not merely a privilege of courtesy, but the real privilege of reminding you—for I am sure I am doing nothing more—of the great principles which we stand associated to promote. I for my part rejoice that we belong to a country in which the whole business of government is so difficult. We do not take orders from anybody; it is a universal communication of conviction, the most subtle, delicate, and difficult of processes. There is not a single individual's opinion that is not of some consequence in making up the grand total, and to be in this great coöperative effort is the most stimulating thing in the world. A man standing alone may well misdoubt his own judgment. He may mistrust his own intellectual processes; he may even wonder if his own heart leads him right in matters of public conduct; but if he finds his heart part of the great throb of a national life, there can be no doubt about it. If that is his happy circumstance, then he may know that he is part of one of the great forces of the world.

I would not feel any exhilaration in belonging to America if I did not feel that she was something more than a rich and powerful nation. I should not feel proud to be in some respects and for a little while her spokesman if I did not believe that there was something else than physical force behind her. I believe that the glory of America is that she is a great spiritual conception and that in the spirit of her institutions dwells not only her distinction but her power. The one thing that the world can not permanently resist is the moral force of great and triumphant convictions.

# THE MEANING OF THE FLAG
## WOODROW WILSON

The following address on the Flag was delivered by President Woodrow Wilson from the south portico of the Treasury Building, Washington, D.C., June 14, 1915.

MR. SECRETARY, FRIENDS, AND FELLOW CITIZENS:—I know of nothing more difficult than to render an adequate tribute to the emblem of our nation. For those of us who have shared that nation's life and felt the beat of its pulse it must be considered a matter of impossibility to express the great things which that emblem embodies. I venture to say that a great many things are said about the flag which very few people stop to analyze. For me the flag does not express a mere body of vague sentiment. The flag of the United States has not been created by rhetorical sentences in declarations of independence and in bills of rights. It has been created by the experience of a great people, and nothing is written upon it that has not been written by their life. It is the embodiment, not of a sentiment, but of a history, and no man can rightly serve under that flag who has not caught some of the meaning of that history.

Experience, ladies and gentlemen, is made by men and women. National experience is the product of those who do the living under that flag. It is their living that has created its significance. You do not create the meaning of a national life by any literary exposition of it, but by the actual daily endeavors of a great people to do the tasks of the day and live up to the ideals of honesty and righteousness and just conduct. And as we think of these things, our tribute is to those men who have created this experience. Many of them are known by name to all the world—statesmen, soldiers, merchants, masters of industry, men of letters and of thought who have coined our hearts into action or into words. Of these men we feel that they have shown us the way. They have not been afraid to go before. They have known that they were speaking the thoughts of a great people when they led that great people along the paths of achievement. There was not a single swashbuckler among them. They were men of sober, quiet thought, the more effective because there was no bluster in it. They were men who thought along the lines of duty, not along the lines of self-aggrandizement. They were men, in short, who thought of the people whom they served and not of themselves.

But while we think of these men and do honor to them as to those who have shown us the way, let us not forget that the real experience and life of a nation lies with the great multitude of unknown men. It lies with those men whose names are never in the headlines of newspapers, those men who know the heat and pain and desperate loss of hope that sometimes comes in the great struggle of daily life; not the men who stand on the side and comment, not the men who merely try to interpret the great struggle, but the men who are engaged in the struggle. They constitute the body of the nation. This flag is the essence of their daily endeavors. This flag does not express any more than what they are and what they desire to be.

As I think of the life of this great nation it seems to me that we sometimes look to the wrong places for its sources. We look to the noisy places, where men are talking in the market place; we look to where men are expressing their individual opinions; we look to where partisans are expressing passions: instead of trying to attune our ears to that voiceless mass of men who merely go about their daily tasks, try to be honorable, try to serve the people they love, try to live worthy of the great communities to which they belong. These are the breath of the nation's nostrils; these are the sinews of its might.

How can any man presume to interpret the emblem of the United States, the emblem of what we would fain be among the family of nations, and find it incumbent upon us to be in the daily round of routine duty? This is Flag Day, but that only means that it is a day when we are to recall the things which we should do every day of our lives. There are no days of special patriotism. There are no days when we should be more patriotic than on other days. We celebrate the Fourth of July merely because the great enterprise of liberty was started on the fourth of July in America, but the great enterprise of liberty was not begun in America. It is illustrated by the blood of thousands of martyrs who lived and died before the great experiment on this side of the water. The Fourth of July merely marks the day when we consecrated ourselves as a nation to this high thing which we pretend to serve. The benefit of a day like this is merely in turning away from the things that distract us, turning away from the things that touch us personally and absorb our interest in the hours of daily work. We remind ourselves of those things that are greater than we are, of those principles by which we believe our hearts to be elevated, of the more difficult things that we must undertake in these days of perplexity when a man's judgment is safest only when it follows the line of principle.

I am solemnized in the presence of such a day. I would not undertake to speak your thoughts. You must interpret them for me. But I do feel that back, not only of every public official, but of every man and woman of the United States, there marches that great host which has brought us to the present day; the host that has never forgotten the vision which it saw at the birth of the nation; the host which always responds to the dictates of humanity and of liberty; the host that will always constitute the strength and the great body of friends of every man who does his duty to the United States.

I am sorry that you do not wear a little flag of the Union every day instead of some days. I can only ask you, if you lose the physical emblem, to be sure that you wear it in your heart, and the heart of America shall interpret the heart of the world.

# MAKERS OF THE FLAG

## FRANKLIN K. LANE

The following address was delivered by the Honorable Franklin
K. Lane, Secretary of the Interior, before the officers and employ-
ees of this Department, about 5,000 in number, at the Inner Court,
Patent Office Building, June 14, 1914.

This morning, as I passed into the Land Office, The Flag dropped me a most
cordial salutation, and from its rippling folds I heard it say: "Good morning, Mr.
Flag Maker."

"I beg your pardon, Old Glory," I said, "aren't you mistaken? I am not the
president of the United States, nor a member of Congress, nor even a general in the
army. I am only a government clerk."

"I greet you again, Mr. Flag Maker," replied the gay voice, "I know you well.
You are the man who worked in the swelter of yesterday straightening out the
tangle of that farmer's homestead in Idaho, or perhaps you found the mistake in
that Indian contract in Oklahoma, or helped to clear that patent for the hopeful in-
ventor in New York, or pushed the opening of that new ditch in Colorado, or made
that mine in Illinois more safe, or brought relief to the old soldier in Wyoming.
No matter; whichever one of these beneficent individuals you may happen to be, I
give you greeting, Mr. Flag Maker."

I was about to pass on, when The Flag stopped me with these words:

"Yesterday the president spoke a word that made happier the future of ten
millions peons in Mexico; but that act looms no larger on the flag than the struggle
which the boy in Georgia is making to win the Corn Club prize this summer.

"Yesterday the Congress spoke a word which will open the door of Alaska;
but a mother in Michigan worked from sunrise until far into the night, to give her
boy an education. She, too, is making the flag.

"Yesterday we made a new law to prevent financial panics, and yesterday,
maybe, a school teacher in Ohio taught his first letters to a boy who will one day
write a song that will give cheer to the millions of our race. We are all making the
flag."

"But," I said impatiently, "these people were only working."

Then came a great shout from The Flag:

"THE WORK that we do is the making of the flag.

"I am not the flag; not at all. I am but its shadow.

"I am whatever you make me, nothing more.

"I am your belief in yourself, your dream of what a people may become.

"I live a changing life, a life of moods and passions, of heartbreaks and tired muscles.

"Sometimes I am strong with pride, when men do an honest work, fitting the rails together truly.

"Sometimes I droop, for then purpose has gone from me, and cynically I play the coward.

"Sometimes I am loud, garish and full of that ego that blasts judgment.

"But always I am all that you hope to be, and have the courage to try for.

"I am song and fear, struggle and panic, and ennobling hope.

"I am the day's work of the weakest man, and the largest dream of the most daring.

"I am the Constitution and the courts, statutes and the statute makers, soldier and dreadnaught, drayman and street sweep, cook, counselor, and clerk.

"I am the battle of yesterday, and the mistake of to-morrow.

"I am the mystery of the men who do without knowing why.

"I am the clutch of an idea, and the reasoned purpose of resolution.

"I am no more than what you believe me to be and I am all that you believe I can be.

"I am what you make me, nothing more.

"I swing before your eyes as a bright gleam of color, a symbol of yourself, the pictured suggestion of that big thing which makes this Nation. My stars and my stripes are your dream and your labors. They are bright with cheer, brilliant with courage, firm with faith, because you have made them so out of your hearts. For you are the makers of the flag and it is well that you glory in the making."

# THE FLAG OF THE UNION FOREVER

## FITZHUGH LEE

Speech of General Fitzhugh Lee at a dinner given by the Friendly Sons of St. Patrick and the Hibernian Society of Philadelphia,
at the city of Philadelphia, September 17, 1887. The occasion of
the dinner was the one hundredth anniversary of the adoption
of the Constitution of the United States. General Lee, then governor of Virginia, was the guest of Governor Beaver at the dinner.
The Chairman, Hon. Andrew G. Curtin [Pennsylvania's war gov-
ernor], in introducing General Lee said: "We have here to-day a
gentleman whom I am glad to call my friend, though during the
war he was in dangerous and unpleasant proximity to me. He
once threatened the capital of this great state. I did not wish him
to come in, and was very glad when he went away. He was then
my enemy and I was his. But, thank God, that is past; and in the
enjoyment of the rights and interests common to all as American
citizens, I am his friend and he is my friend. I introduce to you,
Governor Fitzhugh Lee."

MR. CHAIRMAN AND GENTLEMEN OF THE HIBERNIAN SOCIETY:—I am very glad,
indeed, to have the honor of being present in this society once more; as it was my
good fortune to enjoy a most pleasant visit here and an acquaintance with the
members of your society last year. My engagements were such to-day that I could
not get here earlier; and just as I was coming in Governor Beaver was making his
excuses because, as he said, he had to go to pick up a visitor whom he was to escort
to the entertainment to be given this evening at the Academy of Music. I am the
visitor whom Governor Beaver is looking for. He could not capture me during the
war, but he has captured me now. I am a Virginian and used to ride a pretty fast
horse, and he could not get close enough to me.

By the way, you have all heard of "George Washington and his little hatchet."
The other day I heard a story that was a little variation upon the original, and I am
going to take up your time for a minute by repeating it to you.

It was to this effect: Old Mr. Washington and Mrs. Washington, the parents of
George, found on one occasion that their supply of soap for the use of the family
at Westmoreland had been exhausted, and so they decided to make some family
soap. They made the necessary arrangements and gave the requisite instructions
to the family servant. After an hour or so the servant returned and reported to

them that he could not make that soap. "Why not," he was asked, "haven't you all the materials?" "Yes," he replied, "but there is something wrong." The old folks proceeded to investigate, and they found they had actually got the ashes of the little cherry tree that George had cut down with his hatchet, and there was no lye in it.

Now, I assure you, there is no "lie" in what I say to you this afternoon, and that is, that I thank God for the sun of the Union which, once obscured, is now again in the full stage of its glory; and that its light is shining over Virginia as well as over the rest of this country. We have had our differences. I do not see, upon reading history, how they could well have been avoided, because they resulted from different constructions of the Constitution, which was the helm of the ship of the republic. Virginia construed it one way. Pennsylvania construed it in another, and they could not settle their differences; so they went to war, and Pennsylvania, I think, probably got a little the best of it.

The sword, at any rate, settled the controversy. But that is behind us. We have now a great and glorious future in front of us, and it is Virginia's duty to do all that she can to promote the honor and glory of this country. We fought to the best of our ability for four years; and it would be a great mistake to assume that you could bring men from their cabins, from their plows, from their houses, and from their families to make them fight as they fought in that contest unless they were fighting for a belief. Those men believed that they had the right construction of the Constitution, and that a state that voluntarily entered the Union could voluntarily withdraw from it. They did not fight for Confederate money. It was not worth ten cents a yard. They did not fight for Confederate rations—you would have had to curtail the demands of your appetite to make it correspond with the size and quality of those rations. They fought for what they thought was a proper construction of the Constitution.

They were defeated. They acknowledged their defeat. They came back to their father's house, and there they are going to stay. But if we are to continue prosperous, if this country, stretching from the gulf to the lakes and from ocean to ocean, is to be mindful of its own best interests, in the future, we will have to make concessions and compliances, we will have to bear with each other and to respect each other's opinions. Then we will find that that harmony will be secured which is as necessary for the welfare of states, as it is for the welfare of individuals.

I have become acquainted with Governor Beaver—I met him in Richmond. You could not make me fight him now. If I had known him before the war, perhaps we would not have got at it. If all the Governors had known each other, and if all the people of different sections had been known to each other, or had been thrown together in business or social communication, the fact would have been recognized at the outset, as it is to-day, that there are just as good men in Maine as there are in Texas, and just as good men in Texas as there are in Maine. Human nature is everywhere the same; and when intestine strifes occur, we will doubtless always be able by a conservative, pacific course to pass smoothly over the rugged, rocky edges, and the old Ship of State will be brought into a safe, commodious, Constitutional harbor with the flag of the Union flying over her, and there it will remain.

# FROM WASHINGTON'S FAREWELL AD-DRESS

## GEORGE WASHINGTON

> The appeal for a perpetual union and obedience to established law, the warning against the evils of partisan politics and against the dangers of entangling foreign alliances made by Washington in this immortal address were never more important than at the present time. They will become more important for each succeeding generation. Let those who would know America's mission make a careful study of this the greatest of state papers.

The unity of government which constitutes you one people is also now dear to you. It is justly so, for it is a main pillar in the edifice of your real independence, the support of your tranquillity at home, your peace abroad, of your safety, of your prosperity, of that very liberty which you so highly prize. But as it is easy to foresee that from different causes and from different quarters much pains will be taken, many artifices employed, to weaken in your minds the conviction of this truth, as this is the point in your political fortress against which the batteries of internal and external enemies will be most constantly and actively (though often covertly and insidiously) directed, it is of infinite moment that you should properly estimate the immense value of your national union to your collective and individual happiness; that you should cherish a cordial, habitual, and immovable attachment to it; accustoming yourselves to think and speak of it as of the palladium of your political safety and prosperity; watching for its preservation with jealous anxiety; discountenancing whatever may suggest even a suspicion that it can in any event be abandoned, and indignantly frowning upon the first dawning of every attempt to alienate any portion of our country from the rest or to enfeeble the sacred ties which now link together the various parts.

For this you have every inducement of sympathy and interest. Citizens by birth or choice of a common country, that country has a right to concentrate your affections. The name of American, which belongs to you in your national capacity, must always exalt the just pride of patriotism more than any appellation derived from local discriminations. With slight shades of difference, you have the same religion, manners, habits, and political principles. You have in a common cause fought and triumphed together. The independence and liberty you possess are the work of joint councils and joint efforts, of common dangers, sufferings, and successes.

But these considerations, however powerfully they address themselves to your sensibility, are greatly outweighed by those which apply more immediately to your interest. Here every portion of our country finds the most commanding motives for carefully guarding and preserving the union of the whole.

The *North*, in an unrestrained intercourse with the *South*, protected by the equal laws of a common government, finds in the productions of the latter great additional resources of maritime and commercial enterprise and precious materials of manufacturing industry. The *South*, in the same intercourse, benefiting by the same agency of the *North*, sees its agriculture grow and its commerce expand. Turning partly into its own channels the seamen of the *North*, it finds its particular navigation invigorated; and while it contributes in different ways to nourish and increase the general mass of the national navigation, it looks forward to the protection of a maritime strength to which itself is unequally adapted. The *East*, in a like intercourse with the *West*, already finds, and in the progressive improvement of interior communications by land and water will more and more find, a valuable vent for the commodities which it brings from abroad or manufactures at home. The *West* derives from the *East* supplies requisite to its growth and comfort, and what is perhaps of still greater consequence, it must of necessity owe the *secure* enjoyment of indispensable *outlets* for its own productions to the weight, influence, and the future maritime strength of the Atlantic side of the Union, directed by an indissoluble community of interest as *one nation*. Any other tenure by which the *West* can hold this essential advantage, whether derived from its own separate strength or from an apostate and unnatural connection with any foreign power, must be intrinsically precarious.

While, then, every part of our country thus feels an immediate and particular interest in union, all the parts combined cannot fail to find in the united mass of means and efforts greater strength, greater resource, proportionably greater security from external danger, a less frequent interruption of their peace by foreign nations, and what is of inestimable value, they must derive from union an exemption from those broils and wars between themselves which so frequently afflict neighboring countries not tied together by the same governments, which their own rivalships alone would be sufficient to produce, but which opposite foreign alliances, attachments, and intrigues would stimulate and embitter. Hence, likewise, they will avoid the necessity of those overgrown military establishments which, under any form of government, are inauspicious to liberty, and which are to be regarded as particularly hostile to republican liberty. In this sense it is that your union ought to be considered as a main prop of your liberty, and that the love of the one ought to endear to you the preservation of the other.

These considerations speak a persuasive language to every reflecting and virtuous mind, and exhibit the continuance of the union as a primary object of patriotic desire. Is there a doubt whether a common government can embrace so large a sphere? Let experience solve it. To listen to mere speculation in such a case were criminal. We are authorized to hope that a proper organization of the whole, with the auxiliary agency of governments for the respective subdivisions, will afford a happy issue to the experiment. It is well worth a fair and full experiment. With such powerful and obvious motives to union affecting all parts of our country, while experience shall not have demonstrated its impracticability, there will always be reason to distrust the patriotism of those who in any quarter may endeavor to weaken its bands.

To the efficacy and permanency of your union a government for the whole is indispensable. No alliances, however strict, between the parts can be an adequate substitute. They must inevitably experience the infractions and interruptions which all alliances in all times have experienced. Sensible of this momentous truth, you have improved upon your first essay by the adoption of a constitution of government better calculated than your former for an intimate union and for the efficacious management of your common concerns. This government, the offspring of our own choice, uninfluenced and unawed, adopted upon full investigation and mature deliberation, completely free in its principles, in the distribution of its powers, uniting security with energy, and containing within itself a provision for its own amendment, has a just claim to your confidence and your support. Respect for its authority, compliance with its laws, acquiescence in its measures, are duties enjoined by the fundamental maxims of true liberty. The basis of our political systems is the right of the people to make and to alter their constitutions of government. But the constitution which at any time exists till changed by an explicit and authentic act of the whole people is sacredly obligatory upon all. The very idea of the power and the right of the people to establish government presupposes the duty of every individual to obey the established government.

All obstructions to the execution of the laws, all combinations and associations, under whatever plausible character, with the real design to direct, control, counteract, or awe the regular deliberation and action of the constituted authorities, are destructive of this fundamental principle and of fatal tendency. They serve to organize faction; to give it an artificial and extraordinary force; to put in the place of the delegated will of the nation the will of a party, often a small but artful and enterprising minority of the community, and, according to the alternate triumphs of different parties, to make the public administration the mirror of the ill-concerted and incongruous projects of faction rather than the organ of consistent and wholesome plans, digested by common counsels and modified by mutual interests.

However combinations or associations of the above description may now and then answer popular ends, they are likely in the course of time and things to become potent engines by which cunning, ambitious, and unprincipled men will be enabled to subvert the power of the people, and to usurp for themselves the reins of government, destroying afterwards the very engines which have lifted them to unjust dominion.

Observe good faith and justice toward all nations. Cultivate peace and harmony with all. Religion and morality enjoin this conduct. And can it be that good policy does not equally enjoin it? It will be worthy of a free, enlightened, and at no distant period a great nation to give to mankind the magnanimous and too novel example of a people always guided by an exalted justice and benevolence. Who can doubt that in the course of time and things the fruits of such a plan would richly repay any temporary advantages which might be lost by a steady adherence to it? Can it be that Providence has not connected the permanent felicity of a nation with its virtue? The experiment, at least, is recommended by every sentiment which ennobles human nature. Alas! is it rendered impossible by its vices?

In the execution of such a plan nothing is more essential than that permanent, inveterate antipathies against particular nations and passionate attachments for others should be excluded, and that in place of them just and amicable feelings toward all should be cultivated. The nation which indulges toward another an habitual hatred or an habitual fondness is in some degree a slave. It is a slave to its animosity or to its affection, either of which is sufficient to lead it astray from its duty and its interest. Antipathy in one nation against another disposes each more readily to offer insult and injury, to lay hold of slight causes of umbrage, and to be haughty and intractable when accidental or trifling occasions of dispute occur.

Hence frequent collisions, obstinate, envenomed, and bloody contests. The nation prompted by ill will and resentment sometimes impels to war the government contrary to the best calculations of policy. The government sometimes participates in the national propensity, and adopts through passion what reason would reject. At other times it makes the animosity of the nation subservient to projects of hostility, instigated by pride, ambition, and other sinister and pernicious motives. The peace often, sometimes perhaps the liberty, of nations has been the victim.

So, likewise, a passionate attachment of one nation for another produces a variety of evils. Sympathy for the favorite nation, facilitating the illusion of an imaginary common interest in cases where no real common interest exists, and infusing into one the enmities of the other, betrays the former into a participation in the quarrels and wars of the latter without adequate inducement or justification. It leads also to concessions to the favorite nation of privileges denied to others, which is apt doubly to injure the nation making the concessions by unnecessarily parting with what ought to have been retained, and by exciting jealousy, ill will, and a disposition to retaliate in the parties from whom equal privileges are withheld; and it gives to ambitious, corrupted, or deluded citizens (who devote themselves to the favorite nation) facility to betray or sacrifice the interests of their own country without odium, sometimes even with popularity, gilding with the appearances of a virtuous sense of obligation, a commendable deference for public opinion, or a laudable zeal for public good the base or foolish compliances of ambition, corruption, or infatuation.

As avenues to foreign influence in innumerable ways, such attachments are particularly alarming to the truly enlightened and independent patriot. How many opportunities do they afford to tamper with domestic factions, to practice the arts of seduction, to mislead public opinion, to influence or awe the public councils! Such an attachment of a small or weak toward a great and powerful nation dooms the former to be the satellite of the latter. Against the insidious wiles of foreign influence (I conjure you to believe me, fellow citizens) the jealousy of a free people ought to be *constantly* awake, since history and experience prove that foreign influence is one of the most baneful foes of republican government. But that jealousy, to be useful, must be impartial, else it becomes the instrument of the very influence to be avoided, instead of a defense against it. Excessive partiality for one foreign nation and excessive dislike of another cause those whom they actuate to see danger only on one side, and serve to veil and even second the arts of influence on the other. Real patriots who may resist the intrigues of the favorite are liable to become suspected and odious, while its tools and dupes usurp the applause and confidence of the people to surrender their interests.

The great rule of conduct for us in regard to foreign nations is, in extending our commercial relations to have with them as little *political* connection as possible. So far as we have already formed engagements let them be fulfilled with perfect good faith. Here let us stop.

Europe has a set of primary interests which to us have none or a very remote relation. Hence she must be engaged in frequent controversies, the causes of which are essentially foreign to our concerns. Hence, therefore, it must be unwise in us to implicate ourselves by artificial ties in the ordinary vicissitudes of her politics or the ordinary combinations and collisions of her friendships or enmities.

Our detached and distant situation invites and enables us to pursue a different course. If we remain one people, under an efficient government, the period is not far off when we may defy material injury from external annoyance; when we may take such an attitude as will cause the neutrality we may at any time resolve upon to be scrupulously respected; when belligerent nations, under the impossibility of making acquisitions upon us, will not lightly hazard the giving us provocation; when we may choose peace or war, as our interest, guided by justice, shall counsel.

Why forego the advantages of so peculiar a situation? Why quit our own to stand upon foreign ground? Why, by interweaving our destiny with that of any part of Europe, entangle our peace and prosperity in the toils of European ambition, rivalship, interest, humor, or caprice?

# WASHINGTON

## JOHN W. DANIEL

Address by John W. Daniel, lawyer, statesman, United States senator from Virginia, delivered in the hall of the House of Representatives, Washington, D. C., at the dedication of the Washington National Monument, February 21, 1885, Mr. Daniel being then a member of the House from Virginia. He was introduced by Senator George F. Edmunds, of Vermont, president pro tempore of the Senate, who occupied the speaker's chair, and presided at the dedicatory exercises.

Mr. President of the United States, Senators, Representatives, Judges, Mr. Chairman, and My Countrymen:—Alone in its grandeur stands forth the character of Washington in history; alone like some peak that has no fellow in the mountain range of greatness.

"Washington," says Guizot, "Washington did the two greatest things which in politics it is permitted to man to attempt. He maintained by peace the independence of his country, which he had conquered by war. He founded a free government in the name of principles of order and by re-establishing their sway."

Washington did indeed do these things. But he did more. Out of disconnected fragments he molded a whole and made it a country. He achieved his country's independence by the sword. He maintained that independence by peace as by war. He finally established both his country and its freedom in an enduring frame of constitutional government, fashioned to make Liberty and Union one and inseparable. These four things together constitute the unexampled achievement of Washington.

The world has ratified the profound remark of Fisher Ames, that "he changed mankind's ideas of political greatness." It has approved the opinion of Edward Everett, that he was "the greatest of good men and the best of great men." It has felt for him, with Erskine, "an awful reverence." It has attested the declaration of Brougham, that "he was the greatest man of his own or of any age." It is matter of fact to-day, as when General Hamilton, announcing his death to the army, said, "The voice of praise would in vain endeavor to exalt a name unrivaled in the lists of true glory." America still proclaims him, as did Colonel Henry Lee, on the floor of the House of Representatives, the man "first in war, first in peace, and first in the hearts of his countrymen." And from beyond the sea the voice of Alfieri, breathing the soul of all lands and peoples, still pronounces the blessing, "Happy are you who have for the sublime and permanent basis of your glory the love of country demonstrated by deeds."

Ye who have unrolled the scrolls that tell the tale of the rise and fall of nations, before whose eyes has moved the panorama of man's struggles, achievements, and progression, find you anywhere the story of one whose life work is more than a fragment of that which in his life is set before you? Conquerors, who have stretched your scepters over boundless territories; founders of empire, who have held your dominions in reign of law; reformers, who have cried aloud in the wilderness of oppression; teachers, who have striven with reason to cast down false doctrine, heresy and schism; statesmen, whose brains have throbbed with mighty plans for the amelioration of human society; scar-crowned Vikings of the sea, illustrious heroes of the land, who have borne the standards of siege and battle—come forth in bright array from your glorious fanes—and would ye be measured by the measure of his stature? Behold you not in him a more illustrious and more venerable presence?

Statesman, Soldier, Patriot, Sage, Reformer of Creeds, Teacher of Truth and Justice, Achiever and Preserver of Liberty—the First of Men—Founder and Savior of his Country, Father of his People—this is he, solitary and unapproachable in his grandeur. Oh! felicitous Providence that gave to America OUR WASHINGTON!

High soars into the sky to-day—higher than the Pyramids or the dome of St. Paul's or St. Peter's—the loftiest and most imposing structure that man has ever reared—high soars into the sky to where

"Earth highest yearns to meet a star,"

the monument which "We the people of the United States" have erected to his memory. It is a fitting monument, more fitting than any statue. For his image could only display him in some one phase of his varied character—as the Commander, the Statesman, the Planter of Mount Vernon, or the Chief Magistrate of his Country. So art has fitly typified his exalted life in yon plain lofty shaft. Such is his greatness, that only by a symbol could it be represented. As Justice must be blind in order to be whole in contemplation, so History must be silent, that by this mighty sign she may unfold the amplitude of her story.

In 1657, while yet "a Cromwell filled the Stuarts' throne," there came to Virginia with a party of Carlists who had rebelled against him John Washington, of Yorkshire, England, who became a magistrate and member of the House of Burgesses, and distinguished himself in Indian warfare as the first colonel of his family on this side of the water. He was the nephew of that Sir Henry Washington who had led the forlorn hope of Prince Rupert at Bristol in 1643, and who, with a starving and mutinous garrison, had defended Worcester in 1649, answering all calls for surrender that he "awaited His Majesty's commands."

And his progenitors had for centuries, running back to the conquest, been men of mark and fair renown. Pride and modesty of individuality alike forbid the seeking from any source of a borrowed lustre, and the Washingtons were never studious or pretentious of ancestral dignities. But "we are quotations from our ancestors," says the philosopher of Concord—and who will say that in the loyalty to conscience and to principle, and to the right of self-determination of what is principle, that the Washingtons have ever shown, whether as loyalist or rebel, was not the germ of that deathless devotion to liberty and country which soon discarded all ancient forms in the mighty stroke for independence?

One hundred and fifty-three years ago, on the banks of the Potomac, in the county of Westmoreland, on a spot marked now only by a memorial stone, of the blood of the people whom I have faintly described, fourth in descent from the Colonel John Washington whom I have named, there was born a son to Augustine and Mary Washington. And not many miles above his birthplace is the dwelling where he lived, and near which he now lies buried.

Borne upon the bosom of that river which here mirrors Capitol dome and monumental shaft in its seaward flow, the river itself seems to reverse its current and bear us silently into the past. Scarce has the vista of the city faded from our gaze when we behold on the woodland height that swells above the waters—amidst walks and groves and gardens—the white porch of that old colonial plantation home which has become the shrine of many a pilgrimage. Contrasting it as there it stands to-day with the marble halls which we have left behind us, we realize the truth of Emerson: "The atmosphere of moral sentiment is a region of grandeur which reduces all material magnificence to toys, yet opens to every wretch that has reason the doors of the Universe."

The quaint old wooden mansion, with the stately but simple old-fashioned mahogany furniture, real and ungarnished; the swords and relics of campaigns and scenes familiar to every schoolboy now; the key of the Bastile hanging in the hall incased in glass, calling to mind Tom Paine's happy expression, "That the principles of the American Revolution opened the Bastile is not to be doubted, therefore the key comes to the right place;" the black velvet coat worn when the farewell address to the Army was made; the rooms all in nicety of preparation as if expectant of the coming host—we move among these memorials of days and men long vanished—we stand under the great trees and watch the solemn river, in its never-ceasing flow, we gaze upon the simple tomb whose silence is unbroken save by the low murmur of the waters or the wild bird's note, and we are enveloped in an atmosphere of moral grandeur which no pageantry of moving men nor splendid pile can generate. Nightly on the plain of Marathon—the Greeks have the tradition—there may yet be heard the neighing of chargers and the rushing shadows of spectral war. In the spell that broods over the sacred groves of Vernon, Patriotism, Honor, Courage, Justice, Virtue, Truth seem bodied forth, the only imperishable realities of man's being.

There emerges from the shades the figure of a youth over whose cradle had hovered no star of destiny, nor dandled a royal crown—an ingenious youth, and one who in his early days gave auguries of great powers. The boy whose strong arm could fling a stone across the Rappahannock; whose strong will could tame the most fiery horse; whose just spirit made him the umpire of his fellows; whose obedient heart bowed to a mother's yearning for her son and laid down the midshipman's warrant in the British Navy which answered his first ambitious dream; the student transcribing mathematical problems, accounts, and business forms, or listening to the soldiers and seamen of vessels in the river as they tell of "hair-breadth 'scapes by flood and field;" the early moralist in his thirteenth year compiling matured "Rules for behavior and conversation;" the surveyor of sixteen, exploring the wilderness for Lord Fairfax, sleeping on the ground, climbing mountains, swimming rivers, killing and cooking his own game, noting in his diary soils, minerals, and locations, and making maps which are models of nice and accurate draughtsmanship; the incipient soldier, studying tactics under Adjutant Muse, and taking lessons in broadsword fence from the old soldier of fortune, Jacob Van Braam; the major and adjutant-general of the Virginia frontier forces at nineteen:—we seem to see him yet as here he stood, a model of manly beauty in his youthful prime, a man in all that makes a man ere manhood's years have been fulfilled, standing on the threshold of a grand career, "hearing his days before him and the trumpet of his life."

The scene changes. Out into the world of stern adventure he passes, taking as naturally to the field and the frontier as the eagle to the air. At the age of twenty-one he is riding from Williamsburg to the French post at Venango, in Western Pennsylvania, on a mission for Governor Dinwiddie, which requires "courage to cope with savages and sagacity to negotiate with white men"—on that mission which Edward Everett recognizes as "the first movement of a military nature which resulted in the establishment of American Independence." At twenty-two he has fleshed his maiden sword, has heard the bullets whistle, and found "something charming in the sound;" and soon he is colonel of the Virginia regiment in the unfortunate affair at Fort Necessity, and is compelled to retreat after losing a sixth of his command. He quits the service on a point of military etiquette and honor, but at twenty-three he reappears as volunteer aide by the side of Braddock in the ill-starred expedition against Fort Duquesne, and is the only mounted officer unscathed in the disaster, escaping with four bullets through his garments, and after having two horses shot under him.

The prophetic eye of Samuel Davies has now pointed him out as "that heroic youth, Colonel Washington, whom I can but hope Providence has hitherto preserved in so signal a manner for some important service to his country;" and soon the prophecy is fulfilled. The same year he is in command of the Virginia frontier forces. Arduous conflicts of varied fortunes are ere long ended, and on the 25th of November, 1759, he marches into the reduced fortress of Fort Duquesne—where Pittsburgh now stands, and the Titans of Industry wage the eternal war of Toil—marches in with the advanced guard of his troops, and plants the British flag over its smoking ruins.

That self-same year Wolfe, another young and brilliant soldier of Britain, has scaled and triumphed on the Heights of Abraham—his flame of valor quenched as it lit the blaze of victory; Canada surrenders; the Seven Years' War is done; the French power in America is broken, and the vast region west of the Alleghenies, from the lakes to the Ohio, embracing its valley and tributary streams, is under the scepter of King George. America has been made whole to the English-speaking race, to become in time the greater Britain.

Thus, building wiser than he knew, Washington had taken no small part in cherishing the seed of a nascent nation.

## WASHINGTON AT MOUNT VERNON

Mount Vernon welcomes back the soldier of twenty-seven, who has become a name. Domestic felicity spreads its charms around him with the "agreeable partner" whom he has taken to his bosom, and he dreams of "more happiness than he has experienced in the wide and bustling world."

Already, ere his sword had found its scabbard, the people of Frederick county had made him their member of the House of Burgesses. And the quiet years roll by as the planter, merchant, and representative superintends his plantation, ships his crops, posts his books, keeps his diary, chases the fox for amusement, or rides over to Annapolis and leads the dance at the Maryland capital—alternating between these private pursuits and serving his people as member of the Legislature and justice of the county court.

But ere long this happy life is broken. The air is electric with the currents of revolution. England has launched forth on the fatal policy of taxing her colonies without their consent. The spirit of liberty and resistance is aroused. He is loth to part with the Mother Land, which he still calls "home." But she turns a deaf ear to reason. The first Colonial Congress is called. He is a delegate, and rides to Philadelphia with Henry and Pendleton. The blow at Lexington is struck. The people rush to arms. The sons of the Cavaliers spring to the side of the sons of the Pilgrims. "Unhappy it is," he says, "that a brother's sword has been sheathed in a brother's breast, and that the once happy plains of America are to be either drenched in blood or inhabited by slaves. Sad alternative! But how can a virtuous man hesitate in his choice?" He becomes Commander-in-Chief of the American forces. After seven years' war he is the deliverer of his country. The old Confederation passes away. The Constitution is established. He is twice chosen President, and will not consent longer to serve.

Once again Mount Vernon's grateful shades receive him, and there—the world-crowned Hero now—he becomes again the simple citizen, wishing for his fellow men "to see the whole world in peace and its inhabitants one band of brothers, striving who could contribute most to the happiness of mankind"—without a wish for himself, but "to live and die an honest man on his farm." A speck of war spots the sky. John Adams, now president, calls him forth as lieutenant-general and commander-in-chief to lead America once more. But the cloud vanishes. Peace reigns. The lark sings at Heaven's gate in the fair morn of the new nation. Serene, contented, yet in the strength of manhood, though on the verge of threescore years and ten, he looks forth—the quiet farmer from his pleasant fields, the loving patriarch from the bowers of home—looks forth and sees the work of his hands established in a free and happy people. Suddenly comes the mortal stroke with severe cold. The agony is soon over. He feels his own dying pulse—the hand relaxes—he murmurs, "It is well;" and Washington is no more.

Washington, the friend of Liberty, is no more!

The solemn cry filled the universe. Amidst the tears of his people, the bowed heads of kings, and the lamentations of the nations, they laid him there to rest upon the banks of the river whose murmurs were his boyhood's music—that river which, rising in mountain fastnesses amongst the grandest works of nature and reflecting in its course the proudest works of man, is a symbol of his history, which in its ceaseless and ever-widening flow is a symbol of his eternal fame.

No sum could now be made of Washington's character that did not exhaust language of its tributes and repeat virtues by all her names. No sum could be made of his achievements that did not unfold the history of his country and its institutions—the history of his age and its progress—the history of man and his destiny to be free. But whether character or achievement be regarded, the riches before us only expose the poverty of praise. So clear was he in his great office that no ideal of the Leader or the Ruler can be formed that does not shrink by the side of the reality. And so has he impressed himself upon the minds of men, that no man can justly aspire to be the chief of a great free people who does not adopt his principles and emulate his example. We look with amazement on such eccentric characters as Alexander, Cæsar, Cromwell, Frederick, and Napoleon; but when the serene face of Washington rises before us mankind instinctively exclaims, "This is the Man for the nations to trust and reverence and for heroes and rulers to copy."

Disinterested patriot, he would receive no pay for his military services. Refusing gifts, he was glad to guide the benefaction of a grateful state to educate the children of his fallen braves in the institution at Lexington which yet bears his name. Without any of the blemishes that mark the tyrant, he appealed so loftily to the virtuous elements in man that he almost created the qualities of which his country needed the exercise; and yet he was so magnanimous and forbearing to the weaknesses of others, that he often obliterated the vices of which he feared the consequence. But his virtue was more than this. It was of that daring, intrepid kind that, seizing principle with a giant's grasp, assumes responsibility at any hazard, suffers sacrifice without pretense of martyrdom, bears calumny without reply, imposes superior will and understanding on all around it, capitulates to no unworthy triumph, but must carry all things at the point of clear and blameless conscience. Scorning all manner of meanness and cowardice, his bursts of wrath at their exhibition heighten our admiration for those noble passions which were kindled by the inspirations and exigencies of virtue.

Great in action as by the council board, the finest horseman and knightliest figure of his time, he seemed designed by nature to lead in those bold strokes which needs must come when the battle lies with a single man—those critical moments of the campaign or the strife when, if the mind hesitates or a nerve flinches, all is lost. We can never forget the passage of the Delaware that black December night, amidst shrieking winds and great upheaving blocks of ice which would have petrified a leader of less hardy mold, and then the fell swoop at Trenton. We behold him as when at Monmouth he turns back the retreating lines, and galloping his white charger along the ranks until he falls, leaps on his Arabian bay, and shouts to his men: "Stand fast, my boys, the Southern troops are coming to support you!" And we hear Lafayette exclaim, "Never did I behold so superb a man!" We see him again at Princeton dashing through a storm of shot to rally the wavering troops; he reins his horse between the contending lines, and cries: "Will you leave your general to the foe?" then bolts into the thickest fray. Colonel Fitzgerald, his aid, drops his reins and pulls his hat down over his eyes that he may not see his chieftain fall, when, through the smoke he reappears waving his hat, cheering on his men, and shouting: "Away, dear Colonel, and bring up the troops; the day is ours." "Cœur de Lion" might have doffed his plume to such a chief, for a great knight was he, who met his foes full tilt in the shock of battle and hurled them down with an arm whose sword flamed with righteous indignation.

As children pore over the pictures in their books where they can read the words annexed to them, so we linger with tingling blood by such inspiring scenes, while little do we reck of those dark hours when the aching head pondered the problems of a country's fate. And yet there is a greater theater in which Washington appears, although not so often has its curtain been uplifted.

For it was as a statesman that Washington was greatest. Not in the sense that Hamilton and Jefferson, Adams and Madison were statesmen; but in a larger sense. Men may marshal armies who cannot drill divisions. Men may marshal nations in storm and travail who have not the accomplishments of their cabinet ministers. Not so versed as they was he in the details of political science. And yet as he studied tactics when he anticipated war, so he studied politics when he saw his civil role approaching, reading the history and examining the principles of ancient and modern confederacies, and making notes of their virtues, defects, and methods of operation.

His pen did not possess the facile play and classic grace of their pens, but his vigorous eloquence had the clear ring of our mother tongue. I will not say that he was so astute, so quick, so inventive as the one or another of them—that his mind was characterized by the vivacity of wit, the rich colorings of fancy, or daring flights of imagination. But with him thought and action like well-trained coursers kept abreast in the chariot race, guided by an eye that never quailed, reined by a hand that never trembled. He had a more infallible discrimination of circumstances and men than any of his contemporaries. He weighed facts in a juster scale, with larger equity, and firmer equanimity. He best applied to them the lessons of experience. With greater ascendancy of character he held men to their appointed tasks; with more inspiring virtue he commanded more implicit confidence. He bore a truer divining-rod, and through a wilderness of contention he alone was the unerring Pathfinder of the People. There can, indeed, be no right conception of Washington that does not accord him a great and extraordinary genius. I will not say he could have produced a play of Shakespeare, or a poem of Milton, handled with Kant the tangled skein of metaphysics, probed the secrecies of mind and matter with Bacon, constructed a railroad or an engine like Stephenson, wooed the electric spark from heaven to earth with Franklin, or walked with Newton the pathways of the spheres. But if his genius were of a different order, it was of as rare and high an order. It dealt with man in the concrete, with his vast concerns of business stretching over a continent and projected into the ages, with his seething passions; with his marvelous exertions of mind, body, and spirit to be free. He knew the materials he dealt with by intuitive perception of the heart of man, by experience and observation of his aspirations and his powers, by reflection upon his complex relations, rights, and duties as a social being. He knew just where, between men and states, to erect the monumental mark to divide just reverence for authority from just resistance to its abuse. A poet of social facts, he interpreted by his deeds the harmonies of justice.

First to perceive, and swift to point out, the defects in the Articles of Confederation, they became manifest to all long before victory crowned the warfare conducted under them. Charged by them with the public defense, Congress could not put a soldier in the field; and charged with defraying expenses, it could not levy a dollar of imposts or taxes. It could, indeed, borrow money with the assent of nine states of the thirteen, but what mockery of finance was that, when the borrower could not command any resource of payment.

The states had indeed put but a scepter of straw in the legislative hand of the Confederation—what wonder that it soon wore a crown of thorns! The paper currency ere long dissolved to nothingness; for four days the army was without food, and whole regiments drifted from the ranks of our hard-pressed defenders. "I see," said Washington, "one head gradually changing into thirteen; I see one army gradually branching into thirteen, which, instead of looking up to Congress as the supreme controlling power, are considering themselves as dependent upon their respective states." While yet his sword could not slumber, his busy pen was warning the statesmen of the country that unless Congress were invested with adequate powers, or should assume them as matter of right, we should become but thirteen states, pursuing local interests, until annihilated in a general crash—the cause would be lost—and the fable of the bundle of sticks applied to us.

In rapid succession his notes of alarm and invocations for aid to Union followed each other to the leading men of the states, North and South. Turning to his own state, and appealing to George Mason, "Where," he exclaimed, "where are our men of abilities? Why do they not come forth and save the country?" He compared the affairs of this great continent to the mechanism of a clock, of which each state was putting its own small part in order, but neglecting the great wheel, or spring, which was to put the whole in motion. He summoned Jefferson, Wythe, and Pendleton to his assistance, telling them that the present temper of the states was friendly to lasting union, that the moment should be improved and might never return, and that "after gloriously and successfully contending against the usurpation of Britain we may fall a prey to our own folly and disputes."

How keen the prophet's ken, that through the smoke of war discerned the coming evil; how diligent the patriot's hand, that amidst awful responsibilities reached futureward to avert it! By almost a miracle the weak Confederation, "a barrel without a hoop," was held together perforce of outside pressure; and soon America was free.

But not yet had beaten Britain concluded peace—not yet had dried the blood of Victory's field, ere "follies and disputes" confounded all things with their Babel tongues and intoxicated liberty gave loose to license. An unpaid army with unsheathed swords clamored around a poverty-stricken and helpless Congress. And grown at last impatient even with their chief, officers high in rank plotted insurrection and circulated an anonymous address, urging it "to appeal from the justice to the fears of government, and suspect the man who would advise to longer forbearance." Anarchy was about to erect the Arch of Triumph—poor, exhausted, bleeding, weeping America lay in agony upon her bed of laurels.

Not a moment did Washington hesitate. He convened his officers, and going before them he read them an address, which, for homethrust argument, magnanimous temper, and the eloquence of persuasion which leaves nothing to be added, is not exceeded by the noblest utterances of Greek or Roman. A nobler than Coriolanus was before them, who needed no mother's or wife's reproachful tears to turn the threatening steel from the gates of Rome. Pausing, as he read his speech, he put on his spectacles and said: "I have grown gray in your service, and now find myself growing blind." This unaffected touch of nature completed the master's spell. The late fomenters of insurrection gathered to their chief with words of veneration—the storm went by—and, says Curtis in his History of the Constitution, "Had the Commander-in-Chief been other than Washington, the land would have been deluged with the blood of civil war."

But not yet was Washington's work accomplished. Peace dawned upon the weary land, and parting with his soldiers, he pleaded with them for union. "Happy, thrice happy, shall they be pronounced," he said, "who have contributed anything in erecting this stupendous fabric of freedom and empire; who have assisted in protecting the rights of human nature, and establishing an asylum for the poor and oppressed of all nations and religions." But still the foundations of the stupendous fabric trembled, and no cement held its stones together. It was then, with that thickening peril, Washington rose to his highest stature. Without civil station to call forth his utterance, impelled by the intrepid impulse of a soul that could not see the hope of a nation perish without leaping into the stream to save it, he addressed the whole People of America in a circular to the governors of the states: "Convinced of the importance of the crisis, silence in me," he said, "would be a crime. I will, therefore, speak the language of freedom and sincerity." He set forth the need of union in a strain that touched the quick of sensibility; he held up the citizens of America as sole lords of a vast tract of continent; he portrayed the fair opportunity for political happiness with which Heaven had crowned them; he pointed out the blessings that would attend their collective wisdom; that mutual concessions and sacrifices must be made; and that supreme power must be lodged somewhere to regulate and govern the general concerns of the Confederate Republic, without which the Union would not be of long duration. And he urged that happiness would be ours if we seized the occasion and made it our own. In this, one of the very greatest acts of Washington, was revealed the heart of the man, the spirit of the hero, the wisdom of the sage—I might almost say the sacred inspiration of the prophet.

But still the wing of the eagle drooped; the gathering storms baffled his sunward flight. Even with Washington in the van, the column wavered and halted—states straggling to the rear that had hitherto been foremost for permanent union, under an efficacious constitution. And while three years rolled by amidst the jargon of sectional and local contentions, "the half-starved government," as Washington depicted it, "limped along on crutches, tottering at every step." And while monarchical Europe with saturnine face declared that the American hope of union was the wild and visionary notion of romance, and predicted that we would be to the end of time a disunited people, suspicious and distrustful of each other, divided and subdivided into petty commonwealths and principalities, lo! the very earth yawned under the feet of America, and in that very region whence had come forth a glorious band of orators, statesmen and soldiers to plead the cause and fight the battles of Independence—lo! the volcanic fires of rebellion burst forth upon the heads of the faithful, and the militia were leveling the guns of the Revolution, against the breasts of their brethren. "What, gracious God! is man?" Washington exclaimed: "It was but the other day that we were shedding our blood to obtain the constitutions under which we live, and now we are unsheathing our swords to overturn them."

But see! there is a ray of hope. Maryland and Virginia had already entered into a commercial treaty for regulating the navigation of the rivers and great bay in which they had common interests, and Washington had been one of the commissioners in its negotiation. And now, at the suggestion of Maryland, Virginia had called on all the states to meet in convention at Annapolis, to adopt commercial regulations for the whole country. Could this foundation be laid, the eyes of the nation-builders foresaw that the permanent structure would ere long rise upon it. But when the day of meeting came no state north of New York or south of Virginia was represented; and in their helplessness those assembled could only recommend a constitutional convention, to meet in Philadelphia in May, 1787, to provide for the exigencies of the situation.

And still thick clouds and darkness rested on the land, and there lowered upon its hopes a night as black as that upon the freezing Delaware; but through the gloom the dauntless leader was still marching on to the consummation of his colossal work, with a hope that never died; with a courage that never faltered; with a wisdom that never yielded that "all is vanity."

It was not permitted the Roman to despair of the republic, nor did he—our chieftain. "It will all come right at last," he said. It did. And now let the historian, Bancroft, speak: "From this state of despair the country was lifted by Madison and Virginia." Again he says: "We come now to a week more glorious for Virginia beyond any in her annals, or in the history of any republic that had ever before existed."

It was that week in which Madison, "giving effect to his own long-cherished wishes, and still earlier wishes of Washington," addressing, as it were, the whole country, and marshaling all the states, warned them "that the crisis had arrived at which the people of America are to decide the solemn question, whether they would, by wise and magnanimous efforts reap the fruits of independence and of union, or whether by giving way to unmanly jealousies and prejudices, or to impartial and transitory interests, they would renounce the blessings prepared for them by the Revolution," and conjuring them "to concur in such further concessions and provisions as may be necessary to secure the objects for which that government was instituted, and make the United States as happy in peace as they had been glorious in war."

In such manner, my countrymen, Virginia, adopting the words of Madison, and moved by the constant spirit of Washington, joined in convoking that Constitutional Convention, in which he headed her delegation, and over which he presided, and whose deliberations resulted in the formation and adoption of that instrument which the premier of Great Britain pronounces "the most wonderful work ever struck off at a given time by the brain and purpose of man."

In such manner the state which gave birth to the Father of his Country, following his guiding genius to the Union, as it had followed his sword through the battles of Independence, placed herself at the head of the wavering column. In such manner America heard and hearkened to the voice of her chief; and now closing ranks, and moving with reanimated step, the thirteen commonwealths wheeled and faced to the front, on the line of the Union, under the sacred ensign of the Constitution.

Thus at last was the crowning work of Washington accomplished. Out of the tempests of war, and the tumults of civil commotion, the ages bore their fruit, and the long yearning of humanity was answered. "Rome to America" is the eloquent inscription on one stone contributed to yon colossal shaft—taken from the ancient Temple of Peace that once stood hard by the palace of the Cæsars. Uprisen from the sea of revolution, fabricated from the ruins of the battered Bastiles, and dismantled palaces of unhallowed power, stood forth now the Republic of republics, the Nation of nations, the Constitution of constitutions, to which all lands and times and tongues had contributed of their wisdom. And the priestess of Liberty was in her holy temple.

When Salamis had been fought and Greece again kept free, each of the victorious generals voted himself to be first in honor; but all agreed that Themistocles was second. When the most memorable struggle for the rights of human nature, of which time holds record, was thus happily concluded in the muniment of their preservation, whoever else was second, unanimous acclaim declared that Washington was first. Nor in that struggle alone does he stand foremost. In the name of the people of the United States, their president, their senators, their representatives, and their judges, do crown to-day with the grandest crown that veneration has ever lifted to the brow of glory, him, whom Virginia gave to America, whom America has given to the world and to the ages, and whom mankind with universal suffrage has proclaimed the foremost of the founders of empire in the first degree of greatness; whom Liberty herself has anointed as the first citizen in the great Republic of Humanity.

Encompassed by the inviolate seas stands to-day the American Republic which he founded—a freer Greater Britain—uplifted above the powers and principalities of the earth, even as his monument is uplifted over roof and dome and spire of the multitudinous city.

Long live the Republic of Washington! Respected by mankind, beloved of all its sons, long may it be the asylum of the poor and oppressed of all lands and religions—long may it be the citadel of that liberty which writes beneath the eagle's folded wings, "We will sell to no man, we will deny to no man, Right and Justice."

Long live the United States of America! Filled with the free, magnanimous spirit, crowned by the wisdom, blessed by the moderation, hovered over by the guardian angel of Washington's example; may they be ever worthy in all things to be defended by the blood of the brave who know the rights of man and shrink not from their assertion—may they be each a column, and altogether, under the Constitution, a perpetual Temple of Peace, unshadowed by a Cæsar's palace, at whose altar may freely commune all who seek the union of Liberty and Brotherhood.

Long live our Country! Oh, long through the undying ages may it stand, far removed in fact as in space from the Old World's feuds and follies, alone in its grandeur and its glory, itself the immortal monument of him whom Providence commissioned to teach man the power of Truth, and to prove to the nations that their Redeemer liveth.

# ABRAHAM LINCOLN

## HENRY WATTERSON

Lecture by Henry Watterson, journalist and orator, editor of the
Louisville, Ky., *Courier Journal* since 1868. This lecture was originally delivered before the Lincoln Club of Chicago, February 12,
1895, and subsequently repeated on many platforms as a lecture.
It has been heard in all parts of the country, but nowhere, with
livelier demonstrations of approval than in the cities of the South
"from Richmond and Charleston to New Orleans and Galveston."

The statesmen in knee breeches and powdered wigs who signed the Declaration of Independence and framed the Constitution—the soldiers in blue-and-buff,
top-boots and epaulets who led the armies of the Revolution—were what we are
wont to describe as gentlemen. They were English gentlemen. They were not all,
nor even generally, scions of the British aristocracy; but they came, for the most
part, of good Anglo-Saxon and Scotch-Irish stock.

The shoe buckle and the ruffled shirt worked a spell peculiarly their own.
They carried with them an air of polish and authority. Hamilton, though of obscure birth and small stature, is represented by those who knew him to have been
dignity and grace personified; and old Ben Franklin, even in woolen hose, and
none too courtier-like, was the delight of the great nobles and fine ladies, in whose
company he made himself as much at home as though he had been born a mar-
quis.

The first half of the Republic's first half century of existence the public men
of America, distinguished for many things, were chiefly and almost universally
distinguished for repose of bearing and sobriety of behavior. It was not until the
institution of African slavery had got into politics as a vital force that Congress
became a bear-garden, and that our law-makers, laying aside their manners with
their small clothes, fell into the loose-fitting habiliments of modern fashion and the
slovenly jargon of partisan controversy. The gentlemen who signed the Declaration and framed the Constitution were succeeded by gentlemen—much like themselves—but these were succeeded by a race of party leaders much less decorous
and much more self-confident; rugged, puissant; deeply moved in all that they
said and did, and sometimes turbulent; so that finally, when the volcano burst
forth flames that reached the heavens, great human bowlders appeared amid the
glare on every side; none of them much to speak of according to rules regnant at
St. James and Versailles; but vigorous, able men, full of their mission and of them-

selves, and pulling for dear life in opposite directions.

There were Seward and Sumner and Chase, Corwin and Ben Wade, Trumbull and Fessenden, Hale and Collamer and Grimes, and Wendell Phillips, and Horace Greeley, our latter-day Franklin. There were Toombs and Hammond, and Slidell and Wigfall, and the two little giants, Douglas and Stephens, and Yancey and Mason, and Jefferson Davis. With them soft words buttered no parsnips, and they cared little how many pitchers might be broken by rude ones. The issue between them did not require a diagram to explain it. It was so simple a child might understand. It read, human slavery against human freedom, slave labor against free labor, and involved a conflict as inevitable as it was irrepressible.

Greek was meeting Greek at last; and the field of politics became almost as sulphurous and murky as an actual field of battle. Amid the noise and confusion, the clashing of intellects like sabers bright, and the booming of the big oratorical guns of the North and the South, now definitely arrayed, there came one day into the Northern camp one of the oddest figures imaginable; the figure of a man who, in spite of an appearance somewhat at outs with Hogarth's line of beauty, wore a serious aspect, if not an air of command, and, pausing to utter a single sentence that might be heard above the din, passed on and for a moment disappeared.

The sentence was pregnant with meaning. The man bore a commission from God on high! He said: "A house divided against itself cannot stand. I believe this Government cannot endure permanently half free and half slave. I do not expect the Union to be dissolved; I do not expect the house to fall; but I do expect it will cease to be divided." He was Abraham Lincoln.

How shall I describe him to you? Shall I do so as he appeared to me, when I first saw him immediately on his arrival in the national capital, the chosen president of the United States, his appearance quite as strange as the story of his life, which was then but half known and half told, or shall I use the words of another and a more graphic wordpainter?

In January, 1861, Colonel A. K. McClure, of Pennsylvania, journeyed to Springfield, Illinois, to meet and confer with the man he had done so much to elect, but whom he had never personally known. "I went directly from the depot to Lincoln's house," says Colonel McClure, "and rang the bell, which was answered by Lincoln, himself, opening the door. I doubt whether I wholly concealed my disappointment at meeting him. Tall, gaunt, ungainly, ill-clad, with a homeliness of manner that was unique in itself, I confess that my heart sank within me as I remembered that this was the man chosen by a great nation to become its ruler in the gravest period of its history. I remember his dress as if it were but yesterday—snuff-colored and slouchy pantaloons; open black vest, held by a few brass buttons; straight or evening dress coat, with tightly fitting sleeves to exaggerate his long, bony arms, all supplemented by an awkwardness that was uncommon among men of intelligence. Such was the picture I met in the person of Abraham Lincoln. We sat down in his plainly furnished parlor and were uninterrupted during the nearly four hours I remained with him, and little by little, as his earnestness, sincerity, and candor were developed in conversation, I forgot all the grotesque qualities which so confounded me when I first greeted him. Before half an hour had passed I learned not only to respect, but, indeed, to reverence the man."

A graphic portrait, truly, and not unlike. I recall him, two months later, a little less uncouth, a little better dressed, but in singularity and in angularity much the same. All the world now takes an interest in every detail that concerned him, or that relates to the weird tragedy of his life and death.

### ABRAHAM LINCOLN IN 1861

And who was this peculiar being, destined in his mother's arms—for cradle he had none—so profoundly to affect the future of humankind? He has told us, himself, in words so simple and unaffected, so idiomatic and direct, that we can neither misread them, nor improve upon them. Writing, in 1859, to one who had asked him for some biographic particulars, Abraham Lincoln said:—

"I was born February 12, 1809, in Hardin County, Kentucky. My parents were both born in Virginia, of undistinguished families—second families, perhaps I should say. My mother, who died in my tenth year, was of a family of the name of Hanks.... My paternal grandfather, Abraham Lincoln, emigrated from Rockingham County, Virginia, to Kentucky about 1781 or 1782, where, a year or two later, he was killed by the Indians, not in battle, but by stealth, when he was laboring to open a farm in the forest.

"My father (Thomas Lincoln) at the death of his father was but six years of age. By the early death of his father, and the very narrow circumstances of his mother, he was, even in childhood, a wandering laboring boy, and grew up literally without education. He never did more in the way of writing than bunglingly to write his own name.... He removed from Kentucky to what is now Spencer County, Indiana, in my eighth year.... It was a wild region, with many bears and other animals still in the woods.... There were some schools, so-called, but no qualification was ever required of a teacher beyond 'readin', writin', and cipherin' to the rule of three.' If a straggler supposed to understand Latin happened to sojourn in the neighborhood he was looked upon as a wizard.... Of course, when I came of age I did not know much. Still, somehow, I could read, write, and cipher to the rule of three. But that was all.... The little advance I now have upon this store of education I have picked up from time to time under the pressure of necessity.

"I was raised to farm work ... till I was twenty-two. At twenty-one I came to Illinois—Macon County. Then I got to New Salem, ... where I remained a year as a sort of clerk in a store. Then came the Black Hawk war; and I was elected captain of a volunteer company, a success that gave me more pleasure than any I have had since. I went into the campaign—was elated—ran for the legislature the same year (1832), and was beaten—the only time I ever have been beaten by the people. The next, and three succeeding biennial elections, I was elected to the Legislature. I was not a candidate afterward. During the legislative period I had studied law and removed to Springfield to practice it. In 1846 I was elected to the lower house of Congress. Was not a candidate for reëlection. From 1849 to 1854, inclusive, practiced law more assiduously than ever before. Always a Whig in politics, and generally on the Whig electoral tickets, making active canvasses. I was losing interest in politics when the repeal of the Missouri Compromise aroused me again.

"If any personal description of me is thought desirable, it may be said that I am in height six feet four inches, nearly; lean in flesh, weighing on an average one hundred and eighty pounds; dark complexion, with coarse black hair and gray eyes. No other marks or brands recollected."

There is the whole story, told by himself, and brought down to the point where he became a figure of national importance.

His political philosophy was expounded in four elaborate speeches; one delivered at Peoria, Illinois, the 16th of October, 1854; one at Springfield, Illinois, the 16th of June, 1858; one at Columbus, Ohio, the 16th of September, 1859, and one the 27th of February, 1860, at Cooper Institute, in the city of New York. Of course Mr. Lincoln made many speeches and very good speeches. But these four, progressive in character, contain the sum total of his creed touching the organic character of the Government and at the same time his party view of contemporary issues. They show him to have been an old-line Whig of the school of Henry Clay, with strong emancipation leanings; a thorough anti-slavery man, but never an extremist or an abolitionist. To the last he hewed to the line thus laid down.

Two or three years ago I referred to Abraham Lincoln—in a casual way—as one "inspired of God." I was taken to task for this and thrown upon my defense. Knowing less then than I know now of Mr. Lincoln, I confined myself to the superficial aspects of the case; to the career of a man who seemed to have lacked the opportunity to prepare himself for the great estate to which he had come, plucked as it were from obscurity by a caprice of fortune.

Accepting the doctrine of inspiration as a law of the universe, I still stand to this belief; but I must qualify it as far as it conveys the idea that Mr. Lincoln was not as well equipped in actual knowledge of men and affairs as any of his contemporaries. Mr. Webster once said that he had been preparing to make his reply to Hayne for thirty years. Mr. Lincoln had been in unconscious training for the presidency for thirty years. His maiden address as a candidate for the Legislature, issued at the ripe old age of twenty-three, closes with these words: "But if the good people in their wisdom shall see fit to keep me in the background, I have been too familiar with disappointment to be very much chagrined." The man who wrote that sentence, thirty years later wrote this sentence: "The mystic chords of memory, stretching from every battlefield and patriot grave to every living heart and hearthstone all over this broad land, will yet swell the chorus of the Union, when again touched, as surely they will be, by the angels of our better nature." Between those two sentences, joined by a kindred, somber thought, flowed a life-current—

"Strong, without rage, without o'erflowing, full,"

pausing never for an instant; deepening whilst it ran, but nowise changing its course or its tones; always the same; calm; patient; affectionate; like one born to a destiny, and, as in a dream, feeling its resistless force.

It is needful to a complete understanding of Mr. Lincoln's relation to the time and to his place in the political history of the country, that the student peruse closely the four speeches to which I have called attention; they underlie all that passed in the famous debate with Douglas; all that their author said and did after he succeeded to the presidency. They stand to-day as masterpieces of popular oratory. But for our present purpose the debate with Douglas will suffice—the most extraordinary intellectual spectacle the annals of our party warfare afford. Lincoln entered the canvass unknown outside the state of Illinois. He closed it renowned from one end of the land to the other.

In that great debate it was Titan against Titan; and, perusing it after the lapse of forty years, the philosophic and impartial critic will conclude which got the better of it, Lincoln or Douglas, much according to his sympathy with the one or the other. Douglas, as I have said, had the disadvantage of riding an ebb tide. But Lincoln encountered a disadvantage in riding a flood tide, which was flowing too fast for a man so conservative and so honest as he was. Thus there was not a little equivocation on both sides foreign to the nature of the two. Both wanted to be frank. Both thought they were being frank. But each was a little afraid of his own logic; each was a little afraid of his own following; and hence there was considerable hair splitting, involving accusations that did not accuse and denials that did not deny. They were politicians, these two, as well as statesmen; they were politicians, and what they did not know about political campaigning was hardly worth knowing. Reverently, I take off my hat to both of them; and I turn down the page; I close the book and lay it on its shelf, with the inward ejaculation, "There were giants in those days."

I am not undertaking to deliver an oral biography of Abraham Lincoln, and shall pass over the events which quickly led up to his nomination and election to the presidency in 1860.

I met the newly elected president the afternoon of the day in the early morning of which he had arrived in Washington. It was a Saturday, I think. He came to the capitol under Mr. Seward's escort, and, among the rest, I was presented to him. His appearance did not impress me as fantastically as it had impressed Colonel McClure. I was more familiar with the Western type than Colonel McClure, and, whilst Mr. Lincoln was certainly not an Adonis, even after prairie ideals, there was about him a dignity that commanded respect.

I met him again the forenoon of the 4th of March in his apartment at Willard's Hotel as he was preparing to start to his inauguration, and was touched by his unaffected kindness; for I came with a matter requiring his immediate attention. He was entirely self-possessed; no trace of nervousness; and very obliging. I accompanied the cortege that passed from the senate chamber to the east portico of the capitol, and, as Mr. Lincoln removed his hat to face the vast multitude in front and below, I extended my hand to receive it, but Judge Douglas, just beside me, reached over my outstretched arm and took the hat, holding it throughout the delivery of the inaugural address. I stood near enough to the speaker's elbow not to obstruct any gestures he might make, though he made but few; and then it was that I began to comprehend something of the power of the man.

He delivered that inaugural address as if he had been delivering inaugural addresses all his life. Firm, resonant, earnest, it announced the coming of a man; of a leader of men; and in its ringing tones and elevated style, the gentlemen he had invited to become members of his political family—each of whom thought himself a bigger man than his master—might have heard the voice and seen the hand of a man born to command. Whether they did or not, they very soon ascertained the fact. From the hour Abraham Lincoln crossed the threshold of the White House to the hour he went thence to his death, there was not a moment when he did not dominate the political and military situation and all his official subordinates.

Always courteous, always tolerant, always making allowance, yet always explicit, his was the master-spirit, his the guiding hand; committing to each of the members of his cabinet the details of the work of his own department; caring nothing for petty sovereignty; but reserving to himself all that related to great policies, the starting of moral forces and the moving of organized ideas.

I want to say just here a few words about Mr. Lincoln's relation to the South and the people of the South.

He was, himself, a Southern man. He and all his tribe were Southerners. Although he left Kentucky when but a child, he was an old child; he never was very young; and he grew to manhood in a Kentucky colony; for what was Illinois in those days but a Kentucky colony, grown since somewhat out of proportion? He was in no sense what we in the South used to call "a poor white." Awkward, perhaps; ungainly, perhaps, but aspiring; the spirit of a hero beneath that rugged exterior; the soul of a prose poet behind those heavy brows; the courage of a lion back of those patient, kindly aspects; and, long before he was of legal age, a leader. His first love was a Rutledge; his wife was a Todd. Let the romancist tell the story of his romance. I dare not. No sadder idyl can be found in all the short and simple annals of the poor.

We know that he was a prose poet; for have we not that immortal prose poem recited at Gettysburg? We know that he was a statesman; for has not time vindicated his conclusions? But the South does not know, except as a kind of hearsay, that he was a friend; the one friend who had the power and the will to save it from itself. He was the one man in public life who could have come to the head of affairs in 1861 bringing with him none of the embittered resentments growing out of the anti-slavery battle. Whilst Seward, Chase, Sumner and the rest had been engaged in hand-to-hand combat with the Southern leaders at Washington, Lincoln, a philosopher and a statesman, had been observing the course of events from afar, and like a philosopher and a statesman. The direst blow that could have been laid upon the prostrate South was delivered by the assassin's bullet that struck him down.

But I digress. Throughout the contention that preceded the war, amid the passions that attended the war itself, not one bitter, proscriptive word escaped the lips of Abraham Lincoln, whilst there was hardly a day that he was not projecting his great personality between some Southern man or woman and danger.

Under the date of February 2, 1848, and from the hall of the House of Representatives at Washington, whilst he was serving as a member of Congress, I find this short note to his law partner at Springfield:—

> "DEAR WILLIAM: I take up my pen to tell you that Mr. Stephens, of Georgia, a little, slim, pale-faced, consumptive man,

with a voice like Logan's (that was Stephen T., not John A.), has just concluded the very best speech of an hour's length I ever heard. My old, withered, dry eyes (he was then not quite thirty-seven years of age) are full of tears yet."

From that time forward he never ceased to love Stephens, of Georgia.

After that famous Hampton Roads conference, when the Confederate commissioners, Stephens, Campbell, and Hunter, had traversed the field of official routine with Mr. Lincoln, the president, and Mr. Seward, the secretary of state, Lincoln, the friend, still the old Whig colleague, though one was now president of the United States and the other vice-president of the Southern Confederacy, took the "slim, pale-faced, consumptive man" aside, and, pointing to a sheet of paper he held in his hand, said: "Stephens, let me write 'Union' at the top of that page, and you may write below it whatever else you please."

In the preceding conversation Mr. Lincoln had intimated that payment for the slaves was not outside a possible agreement for reunion and peace. He based that statement upon a plan he already had in hand, to appropriate four hundred millions of dollars to this purpose.

There are those who have put themselves to the pains of challenging this statement of mine. It admits of no possible equivocation. Mr. Lincoln carried with him to Fortress Monroe two documents that still stand in his own handwriting; one of them a joint resolution to be passed by the two houses of Congress appropriating the four hundred millions, the other a proclamation to be issued by himself, as president, when the joint resolution had been passed. These formed no part of the discussion at Hampton Roads, because Mr. Stephens told Mr. Lincoln they were limited to treating upon the basis of the recognition of the Confederacy, and to all intents and purposes the conference died before it was actually born. But Mr. Lincoln was so filled with the idea that next day, when he had returned to Washington, he submitted the two documents to the members of his cabinet. Excepting Mr. Seward, they were all against him. He said: "Why, gentlemen, how long is the war going to last? It is not going to end this side of a hundred days, is it? It is costing us four millions a day. There are the four hundred millions, not counting the loss of life and property in the meantime. But you are all against me, and I will not press the matter upon you." I have not cited this fact of history to attack, or even to criticize, the policy of the Confederate Government, but simply to illustrate the wise magnanimity and justice of the character of Abraham Lincoln. For my part I rejoice that the war did not end at Fortress Monroe — or any other conference — but that it was fought out to its bitter and logical conclusion at Appomattox.

It was the will of God that there should be, as God's own prophet had promised, "a new birth of freedom," and this could only be reached by the obliteration of the very idea of slavery. God struck Lincoln down in the moment of his triumph, to attain it; He blighted the South to attain it. But He did attain it. And here we are this night to attest it. God's will be done on earth as it is done in Heaven. But let no Southern man point finger at me because I canonize Abraham Lincoln, for he was the one friend we had at court when friends were most in need; he was the one man in power who wanted to preserve us intact, to save us from the wolves of passion and plunder that stood at our door; and as that God, of whom it has been said that "whom He loveth He chasteneth," meant that the South should be chastened, Lincoln was put out of the way by the bullet of an assassin, having neither lot nor parcel, North or South, but a winged emissary of fate, flown from the shadows of the mystic world, which Æschylus and Shakespeare created and consecrated to tragedy!

I sometimes wonder shall we ever attain a journalism sufficiently upright in its treatment of current events to publish fully and fairly the utterances of our public men, and, except in cases of provable dishonor, to leave their motives and their personalities alone?

Reading just what Abraham Lincoln did say and did do, it is inconceivable how such a man could have aroused antagonism so bitter and abuse so savage, to fall at last by the hand of an assassin.

We boast our superior civilization and our enlightened freedom of speech; and yet, how few of us—when a strange voice begins to utter unfamiliar or unpalatable things—how few of us stop and ask ourselves, may not this man be speaking the truth after all? It is so easy to call names. It is so easy to impugn motives. It is so easy to misrepresent opinions we cannot answer. From the least to the greatest what creatures we are of party spirit, and yet, for the most part, how small its aims, how imperfect its instruments, how disappointing its conclusions!

One thinks now that the world in which Abraham Lincoln lived might have dealt more gently by such a man. He was himself so gentle—so upright in nature and so broad of mind—so sunny and so tolerant in temper—so simple and so unaffected in bearing—a rude exterior covering an undaunted spirit, proving by his every act and word that—

> "The bravest are the tenderest,
> The loving are the daring."

Though he was a party leader, he was a typical and patriotic American, in whom even his enemies might have found something to respect and admire. But it could not be so. He committed one grievous offense; he dared to think and he was not afraid to speak; he was far in advance of his party and his time; and men are slow to forgive what they do not readily understand.

Yet, all the while that the waves of passion were dashing over his sturdy figure, reared above the dead-level, as a lone oak upon a sandy beach, not one harsh word rankled in his heart to sour the milk of human kindness that, like a perennial spring from the gnarled roots of some majestic tree, flowed within him. He would smooth over a rough place in his official intercourse with a funny story fitting the case in point, and they called him a trifler. He would round off a logical argument with a familiar example, hitting the nail squarely on the head and driving it home, and they called him a buffoon. Big wigs and little wigs were agreed that he lowered the dignity of debate; as if debates were intended to mystify, and not to clarify truth. Yet he went on and on, and never backward, until his time was come, when his genius, fully developed, rose to the great exigencies intrusted to his hands. Where did he get his style? Ask Shakespeare and Burns where they got their style. Where did he get his grasp upon affairs and his knowledge of men? Ask the Lord God who created miracles in Luther and Bonaparte!

What was the mysterious power of this mysterious man, and whence?

His was the genius of common sense; of common sense in action; of common sense in thought; of common sense enriched by experience and unhindered by fear. "He was a common man," says his friend Joshua Speed, "expanded into giant proportions; well acquainted with the people, he placed his hand on the beating pulse of the nation, judged of its disease, and was ready with a remedy." Inspired he was truly, as Shakespeare was inspired; as Mozart was inspired; as Burns was inspired; each, like him, sprung directly from the people.

I look into the crystal globe that, slowly turning, tells the story of his life, and I see a little heart broken boy, weeping by the outstretched form of a dead mother, then bravely, nobly trudging a hundred miles to obtain her Christian burial. I see this motherless lad growing to manhood amid the scenes that seem to lead to nothing but abasement; no teachers; no books; no chart, except his own untutored mind; no compass, except his own undisciplined will; no light, save light from Heaven; yet, like the caravel of Columbus, struggling on and on through the trough of the sea, always toward the destined land. I see the full-grown man, stalwart and brave, an athlete in activity of movement and strength of limb, yet vexed by weird dreams and visions; of life, of love, of religion, sometimes verging on despair. I see the mind, grown as robust as the body, throw off these phantoms of the imagination and give itself wholly to the work-a-day uses of the world; the rearing of children; the earning of bread; the multiplied duties of life. I see the party leader, self-confident in conscious rectitude; original, because it was not his nature to follow; potent, because he was fearless, pursuing his convictions with earnest zeal, and urging them upon his fellows with the resources of an oratory which was hardly more impressive than it was many-sided. I see him, the preferred among his fellows, ascend the eminence reserved for him, and him alone of all the statesmen of the time, amid the derision of opponents and the distrust of supporters, yet unawed and unmoved, because thoroughly equipped to meet the emergency. The same being, from first to last; the poor child weeping over a dead mother; the great chief sobbing amid the cruel horrors of war; flinching not from duty, nor changing his life-long ways of dealing with the stern realities which pressed upon him and hurried him onward. And, last scene of all, that ends this strange, eventful history, I see him lying dead there in the capitol of the nation, to which he had rendered "the last, full measure of his devotion," the flag of his country around him, the world in mourning, and, asking myself how could any man have hated that man, I ask you, how can any man refuse his homage to his memory? Surely, he was one of God's elect; not in any sense a creature of circumstance, or accident. Recurring to the doctrine of inspiration, I say again and again, he was inspired of God, and I cannot see how any one who believes in that doctrine can regard him as anything else.

From Cæsar to Bismarck and Gladstone the world has had its statesmen and its soldiers—men who rose to eminence and power step by step, through a series of geometric progression as it were, each advancement following in regular order one after the other, the whole obedient to well-established and well-understood laws of cause and effect. They were not what we call "men of destiny." They were "men of the time." They were men whose careers had a beginning, a middle and an end, rounding off lives with histories, full it may be of interesting and exciting event, but comprehensive and comprehensible; simple, clear, complete.

The inspired ones are fewer. Whence their emanation, where and how they got their power, by what rule they lived, moved and had their being, we know not. There is no explication to their lives. They rose from shadow and they went in mist. We see them, feel them, but we know them not. They came, God's word upon their lips; they did their office, God's mantle about them; and they vanished, God's holy light between the world and them, leaving behind a memory, half mortal and half myth. From first to last they were the creations of some special Providence, baffling the wit of man to fathom, defeating the machinations of the world, the flesh and the devil, until their work was done, then passing from the scene as mysteriously as they had come upon it.

Tried by this standard, where shall we find an example so impressive as Abraham Lincoln, whose career might be chanted by a Greek chorus as at once the prelude and the epilogue of the most imperial theme of modern times?

Born as lowly as the Son of God, in a hovel; reared in penury, squalor, with no gleam of light or fair surrounding; without graces, actual or acquired; without name or fame or official training; it was reserved for this strange being, late in life, to be snatched from obscurity, raised to supreme command at a supreme moment, and intrusted with the destiny of a nation.

The great leaders of his party, the most experienced and accomplished public men of the day, were made to stand aside; were sent to the rear, whilst this fantastic figure was led by unseen hands to the front and given the reins of power. It is immaterial whether we were for him, or against him; wholly immaterial. That, during four years, carrying with them such a weight of responsibility as the world never witnessed before, he filled the vast space allotted him in the eyes and actions of mankind, is to say that he was inspired of God, for nowhere else could he have acquired the wisdom and the virtue.

Where did Shakespeare get his genius? Where did Mozart get his music? Whose hand smote the lyre of the Scottish plowman, and stayed the life of the German priest? God, God, and God alone; and as surely as these were raised up by God, inspired by God, was Abraham Lincoln; and a thousand years hence, no drama, no tragedy, no epic poem will be filled with greater wonder, or be followed by mankind with deeper feeling than that which tells the story of his life and death.

# SECOND INAUGURAL ADDRESS
## ABRAHAM LINCOLN

Delivered by Abraham Lincoln, March 4, 1865, on the occasion of
his second inauguration as president of the United States.

FELLOW COUNTRYMEN:—At this second appearing to take the oath of the presidential office, there is less occasion for an extended address than there was at the first. Then a statement, somewhat in detail, of a course to be pursued, seemed fitting and proper. Now, at the expiration of four years, during which public declarations have been constantly called forth on every point and phase of the great contest, which still absorbs the attention and engrosses the energies of the nation, little that is new could be presented. The progress of our arms, upon which all else chiefly depends, is as well known to the public as to myself; and it is, I trust, reasonably satisfactory and encouraging to all. With high hope for the future, no prediction in regard to it is ventured.

On the occasion corresponding to this four years ago all thoughts were anxiously directed to an impending civil war. All dreaded it—all sought to avert it. While the inaugural address was being delivered from this place, devoted altogether to saving the Union without war, insurgent agents were in the city seeking to destroy it without war—seeking to dissolve the Union, and divide effects, by negotiation. Both parties deprecated war; but one of them would make war rather than let the nation survive; and the other would accept war rather than let it perish. And the war came.

One eighth of the whole population were colored slaves, not distributed generally over the Union, but localized in the Southern part of it. These slaves constituted a peculiar and powerful interest. All knew that this interest was, somehow, the cause of the war. To strengthen, perpetuate, and extend this interest was the object for which insurgents would rend the Union, even by war; while the government claimed no right to do more than to restrict the territorial enlargement of it.

Neither party expected for the war the magnitude or the duration which it has already attained. Neither anticipated that the cause of the conflict might cease with, or even before, the conflict itself should cease. Each looked for an easier triumph, and a result less fundamental and astounding. Both read the same Bible, and pray to the same God; and each invokes his aid against the other. It may seem strange that any men should dare to ask a just God's assistance in wringing their bread from the sweat of other men's faces; but let us judge not, that we be not judged. The prayers of both could not be answered—that of neither has been answered fully.

The Almighty has his own purposes. "Woe unto the world because of offenses! for it must needs be that offenses come; but woe to that man by whom the offense cometh." If we shall suppose that American slavery is one of those offenses which, in the providence of God, must needs come, but which, having continued through his appointed time, he now wills to remove, and that he gives to both North and South this terrible war, as the woe due to those by whom the offense came, shall we discern therein any departure from those divine attributes which the believers in a living God always ascribe to him? Fondly do we hope—fervently do we pray—that this mighty scourge of war may speedily pass away. Yet, if God wills that it continue until all the wealth piled by the bondman's two hundred and fifty years of unrequited toil shall be sunk, and until every drop of blood drawn with the lash shall be paid by another drawn with the sword, as was said three thousand years ago, so still it must be said, "The judgments of the Lord are true and righteous altogether."

With malice toward none; with charity for all; with firmness in the right, as God gives us to see the right, let us strive on to finish the work we are in; to bind up the nation's wounds; to care for him who shall have borne the battle, and for his widow and his orphan—to do all which may achieve and cherish a just and lasting peace among ourselves and with all nations.

# ROBERT E. LEE

## E. BENJAMIN ANDREWS

The following extracts are taken from the great lecture[22] of E. Benjamin Andrews on "Robert E. Lee." Dr. Andrews was president of Brown University 1889-1898, superintendent of the Public Schools of Chicago 1898-1900, chancellor of the University of Nebraska 1900-1908, and since 1909 has been chancellor emeritus of that institution. He served as a private, and later as second lieutenant in the Union army during the Civil War. He was wounded at Petersburg, losing an eye. Probably no better characterization or higher tribute has ever been made of Robert E. Lee than that by Dr. Andrews in this lecture which was as enthusiastically received by the Union veterans of the North as by the Confederate veterans of the South; for, as Dr. Andrews says in his tribute to Lee, "None are prouder of his record than those who fought against him, who while recognizing the purity of his motive, thought him in error in going from under the stars and stripes."

Robert Edward Lee had perhaps a more illustrious traceable lineage than any American not of his family. His ancestor, Lionel Lee, crossed the English Channel with William the Conqueror. Another scion of the clan fought beside Richard the Lion-hearted at Acre in the Third Crusade. To Richard Lee, the great land owner on Northern Neck, the Virginia Colony was much indebted for royal recognition. His grandson, Henry Lee, was the grandfather of "Light-horse Harry" Lee of Revolutionary fame, who was the father of Robert Edward Lee.

Robert E. Lee was born on January 19, 1807, in Westmoreland County, Va., the same county that gave to the world George Washington and James Monroe. Though he was fatherless at eleven, the father's blood in him inclined him to the profession of arms, and when eighteen,—in 1825,—on an appointment obtained for him by General Andrew Jackson, he entered the Military Academy at West Point. He graduated in 1829, being second in rank in a class of forty-six. Among his classmates were two men whom one delights to name with him—Ormsby M. Mitchel, later a general in the Federal army, and Joseph E. Johnston, the famous Confederate. Lee was at once made Lieutenant of Engineers, but, till the Mexican War, attained only a captaincy. This was conferred on him in 1838.

[22] This lecture is found in full in Vol. XII (1915 Edition) of "Beacon Lights of History," copyright 1902 by the publishers, Fords, Howard & Hulbert, and is here used by special permission of Dr. Andrews and his publishers.

In 1831 Lee had been married to Miss Mary Randolph Custis, the grand daughter of Mrs. George Washington. By this marriage he became possessor of the beautiful estate at Arlington, opposite Washington, his home till the Civil War. The union, blessed by seven children, was in all respects most happy.

In his prime Lee was spoken of as the handsomest man in the army. He was about six feet high, perfectly built, healthy, fond of outdoor life, enthusiastic in his profession, gentle, dignified, studious, broad-minded, and positively, though unobtrusively, religious. If he had faults, which those nearest him doubted, they were excess of modesty and excess of tenderness.

During the Mexican War, Captain Lee directed all the most important engineering operations of the American army—a work vital to its wonderful success. Already at the siege of Vera Cruz, General Scott mentioned him as having "greatly distinguished himself." He was prominent in all the operations thence to Cerro Gordo, where, in April, 1847, he was brevetted major. Both at Contreras and at Churubusco he was credited with gallant and meritorious services. At the charge up Chapultepec, in which Joseph E. Johnston, George B. McClellan, George E. Pickett, and Thomas J. Jackson participated, Lee bore Scott's orders to all points until from loss of blood by a wound, and from the loss of two nights' sleep at the batteries, he actually fainted away in the discharge of his duty. Such ability and devotion brought him home from Mexico bearing the brevet rank of colonel. General Scott had learned to think of him as "the greatest military genius in America."

In 1852 Lee was made superintendent of the West Point Military Academy. In 1855 he was commissioned lieutenant-colonel of Col. Albert Sidney Johnston's new cavalry regiment, just raised to serve in Texas. March, 1861, saw him colonel of the First United States Cavalry. With the possible exception of the two Johnstons, he was now the most promising candidate for General Scott's position whenever that venerable hero vacated it, as he was sure to do soon.

Lee was a Virginian, and Virginia, about to secede and at length seceding, in most earnest tones besought her distinguished son to join her. It seemed to him the call of duty, and that call, as he understood it, was one which it was not in him to disobey. President Lincoln knew the value of the man, and sent Frank Blair to him to say that if he would abide by the Union he should soon command the whole active army. That would probably have meant his election, in due time, to the presidency of his country. "For God's sake don't resign, Lee!" General Scott—himself a Virginian—is said to have pleaded. He replied: "I am compelled to; I cannot consult my own feelings in the matter." Accordingly, three days after Virginia passed its ordinance of secession, Lee sent to Simon Cameron, Secretary of War, his resignation as an officer in the United States army.

Few at the North were able to understand the secession movement, most denying that a man at once thoughtful and honorable could join in it. So centralized had the North by 1861 become in all social and economic particulars, that centrality in government was taken as a matter of course. Representing this, the nation was deemed paramount to any state. Governmental sovereignty, like travel and trade, had come to ignore state lines. The whole idea and feeling of state sovereignty, once as potent North as South, had vanished and been forgotten.

Far otherwise at the South, where, owing to the great size of states and to the paucity of railways and telegraphs, interstate association was not yet a force. Each state, being in square miles ample enough for an empire, retained to a great extent the consciousness of an independent nation. The state was near and palpable; the central government seemed a vague and distant thing. Loyalty was conceived as binding one primarily to one's own state.

It is a misconception to explain this feeling—for in most cases it was feeling rather than reasoned conviction—by Calhoun's teaching. It resulted from geography and history, and, these factors working as they did, would have been what it was had Calhoun never lived. These considerations explain how Colonel Lee, certainly one of the most conscientious men who ever lived, felt bound in duty and honor to side with seceding Virginia, though he doubted the wisdom of her course.

Most striking among the characteristics of General Lee which made him so successful was his exalted and unmatched excellence as a man, his unselfishness, sweetness, gentleness, patience, love of justice, and general elevation of soul. Lee much loved to quote Sir William Hamilton's words: "On earth nothing great but man: in man nothing great but mind." He always added, however: "In mind nothing great save devotion to truth and duty." Though a soldier, and at last very eminent as a soldier, he retained from the beginning to the end of his career the entire temper and character of an ideal civilian. He did not sink the man in the military man. He had all a soldier's virtues, the "chevalier without fear and without reproach," but he was glorified by a whole galaxy of excellences which soldiers too often lack. He was pure of speech and of habit, never intemperate, never obscene, never profane, never irreverent. In domestic life he was an absolute model. Lofty command did not make him vain.

That Lee was brave need not be said. He was not as rash as Hood and Cleburne sometimes were. He knew the value of his life to the great cause, and, usually at least, did not expose himself needlessly. Prudence he had, but no fear. His resolution to lead the charge at the Bloody Angle—rashness at once—shows fearlessness. Tender-hearted as he was, Lee felt battle frenzy as hardly another great commander ever did. From him it spread like magnetism to his officers and men, thrilling all as if the chief himself were close by in the fray, shouting, "Now fight, my good fellows, fight!" Yet such was Lee's self-command that this ardor never carried him too far.

But Lee possessed another order of courage infinitely higher and rarer than this—the sort so often lacking even in generals who have served with utmost distinction in high subordinate places, when they are called to the sole and decisive direction of armies: he had that royal mettle, that preternatural decision of character, ever tempered with caution and wisdom, which leads a great commander, when true occasion arises, resolutely to give general battle, or a swing out away from his base upon a precarious but promising campaign. Here you have moral heroism; ordinary valor is more impulsive. A weaker man, albeit total stranger to fear, ready to lead his division or his corps into the very mouth of hell, if commanded, being set himself to direct an army, will be either rash or else too timid, or fidget from one extreme to the other, losing all.

ROBERT E. LEE

It was in this supreme kind of boldness that Robert Lee preëminently excelled. Cautious always, he still took risks and responsibilities which common generals would not have dared to take, and when he had assumed these, his mighty will forbade him to sink under the load. The braying of bitter critics, the obloquy of men who should have supported him, the shots from behind, dismayed him no more than did Burnside's cannon at Fredericksburg. On he pressed, stout as a Titan, relentless as fate. What time bravest hearts failed at victory's delay, this Dreadnaught rose to his best, and furnished courage for the whole Confederacy.

In a sense, of course, the cause for which Lee fought was "lost"; yet a very great part of what he and his *confreres* sought, the war actually secured and assured. His cause was not "lost" as Hannibal's was, whose country, with its institutions, spite of his genius and devotion, utterly perished from the earth. Yet Hannibal is remembered more widely than Scipio. Were Lee in the same case with Hannibal, men would magnify his name as long as history is read. "Of illustrious men," says Thucydides, "the whole earth is the sepulcher. They are immortalized not alone by columns and inscriptions in their own lands; memorials to them rise in foreign countries as well—not of stone, it may be, but unwritten, in the thoughts of posterity."

Lee's case resembles Cromwell's much more than Hannibal's. The *regime* against which Cromwell warred returned in spite of him; but it returned modified, involving all the reforms for which the chieftain had bled. So the best of what Lee drew sword for is here in our actual America, and, please God, shall remain here forever.

Decisions of the United States Supreme Court since Secession gave a sweep and a certainty to the rights of states and limit the central power in this republic as had never been done before. The wild doctrines of Sumner and Thaddeus Stevens on these points are not our law. If the Union is perpetual, equally so is each state. The republic is "an indestructible Union of indestructible states." If this part of our law had in 1861 received its present definition and emphasis, and if the Southern States had then been sure, come what might, of the freedom they actually now enjoy each to govern itself in its own way, even South Carolina might never have voted secession. And inasmuch as the war, better than aught else could have done, forced this phase of the Constitution out into clear expression, General Lee did not fight in vain. The essential good he wished has come, while the republic with its priceless benedictions to us all remains intact. All Americans thus have part in Robert Lee, not only as a peerless man and soldier, but as the sturdy miner, sledge-hammering the rock of our liberties till it give forth its gold. None are prouder of his record than those who fought against him, who, while recognizing the purity of his motive, thought him in error in going from under the stars and stripes. It is likely that more American hearts day by day think lovingly of Lee than of any other Civil War celebrity save Lincoln alone. And his praise will increase.

# OUR REUNITED COUNTRY

## CLARK HOWELL

Speech of Clark Howell at the Peace Jubilee Banquet in Chicago,
October 19, 1898, in response to the toast "Our Reunited Country: North and South."

MR. TOASTMASTER, AND MY FELLOW COUNTRYMEN:—In the mountains of my
state, in a county remote from the quickening touch of commerce, and railroads
and telegraphs—so far removed that the sincerity of its rugged people flows un-
polluted from the spring of nature—two vine-covered mounds, nestling in the
solemn silence of a country churchyard, suggest the text of my response to the
sentiment to which I am to speak to-night. A serious text, Mr. Toastmaster, for an
occasion like this, and yet out of it there is life and peace and hope and prosperity, for in the solemn sacrifice of the voiceless grave can the chiefest lesson of the
Republic be learned, and the destiny of its real mission be unfolded. So, bear with
me while I lead you to the rust-stained slab, which for a third of a century—since
Chickamauga—has been kissed by the sun as it peeped over the Blue Ridge, melt-
ing the tears with which the mourning night had bedewed the inscription:—

> "Here lies a Confederate soldier.
> He died for his country."

The September day which brought the body of this mountain hero to that
home among the hills which had smiled upon his infancy, been gladdened by
his youth, and strengthened by his manhood, was an ever memorable one with
the sorrowing concourse of friends and neighbors who followed his shot-riddled
body to the grave. And of that number no man gainsaid the honor of his death,
lacked full loyalty to the flag for which he fought, or doubted the justice of the
cause for which he gave his life.

Thirty-five years have passed; another war has called its roll of martyrs; again
the old bell tolls from the crude latticed tower of the settlement church; another
great pouring of sympathetic humanity, and this time the body of a son, wrapped
in the stars and stripes, is lowered to its everlasting rest beside that of the father
who sleeps in the stars and bars.

There were those there who stood by the grave of the Confederate hero years
before, and the children of those were there, and of those present no one gainsaid
the honor of the death of this hero of El Caney, and none were there but loved, as
patriots alone can love, the glorious flag that enshrines the people of a common
country as it enshrouds the form that will sleep forever in its blessed folds. And on

this tomb will be written:

> "Here lies the son of a Confederate soldier,
> He died for his country."

And so it is that between the making of these two graves human hands and human hearts have reached a solution of the vexed problem that has baffled human will and human thought for three decades. Sturdy sons of the South have said to their brothers of the North that the people of the South had long since accepted the arbitrament of the sword to which they had appealed. And likewise the oft-repeated message has come back from the North that peace and good will reigned, and that the wounds of civil dissention were but as sacred memories. Good fellowship was wafted on the wings of commerce and development from those who had worn the blue to those who had worn the gray. Nor were these messages delivered in vain, for they served to pave the way for the complete and absolute elimination of the line of sectional differences by the only process by which such a result was possible. The sentiment of the great majority of the people of the South was rightly spoken in the message of the immortal Hill, and in the burning eloquence of Henry Grady—both Georgians—the record of whose blessed work for the restoration of peace between the sections becomes a national heritage, and whose names are stamped in enduring impress upon the affection of the people of the Republic.

And yet there were still those among us who believed your course was polite, but insincere, and those among you who assumed that our professed attitude was sentimental and unreal. Bitterness had departed, and sectional hate was no more, but there were those who feared, even if they did not believe, that between the great sections of our greater government there was not the perfect faith and trust and love that both professed; that there was want of the faith that made the American Revolution a successful possibility; that that there was want of the trust that crystallized our States into the original Union; that there was lack of the love that bound in unassailable strength the united sisterhood of States that withstood the shock of Civil War. It is true this doubt existed to a greater degree abroad than at home. But to-day the mist of uncertainty has been swept away by the sunlight of events, and there, where doubt obscured before stands in bold relief, commanding the admiration of the whole world, the most glorious type of united strength and sentiment and loyalty known to the history of nations.

Out of the chaos of that civil war had risen a new nation, mighty in the vastness of its limitless resources, the realities within its reach surpassing the dreams of fiction, and eclipsing the fancy of fable—a new nation, yet rosy in the flesh, with the bloom of youth upon its cheeks and the gleam of morning in its eyes. No one questioned that commercial and geographic union had been effected. So had Rome reunited its faltering provinces, maintaining the limit of its imperial jurisdiction by the power of commercial bonds and the majesty of the sword, until in its very vastness it collapsed. The heart of its people did not beat in unison. Nations may be made by the joining of hands, but the measure of their real strength and vitality, like that of the human body, is in the heart. Show me the country whose people are not at heart in sympathy with its institutions, and the fervor of whose patriotism is not bespoken in its flag, and I will show you a ship of state which is sailing in shallow waters, toward unseen eddies of uncertainty, if not to the open rocks of dismemberment.

Whence was the proof to come, to ourselves as well as to the world, that we were being moved once again by a common impulse, and by the same heart that inspired and gave strength to the hands that smote the British in the days of the Revolution, and again at New Orleans; that made our ships the masters of the seas; that placed our flag on Chapultepec, and widened our domain from ocean to ocean? How was the world to know that the burning fires of patriotism, so essential to national glory and achievement, had not been quenched by the blood spilled by the heroes of both sides of the most desperate struggle known in the history of civil wars? How was the doubt that stood, all unwilling, between outstretched hands and sympathetic hearts, to be, in fact, dispelled?

If from out the caldron of conflict there arose this doubt, only from the crucible of war could come the answer. And, thank God, that answer has been made in the record of the war, the peaceful termination of which we celebrate to-night. Read it in every page of its history; read it in the obliteration of party and sectional lines in the congressional action which called the nation to arms in the defense of prostrate liberty, and for the extension of the sphere of human freedom; read it in the conduct of the distinguished Federal soldier who, as the chief executive of this great republic,[23] honors this occasion by his presence to-night, and whose appointments in the first commissions issued after war had been declared made manifest the sincerity of his often repeated utterances of complete sectional reconciliation and the elimination of sectional lines in the affairs of government. Differing with him, as I do, on party issues, utterly at variance with the views of his party on economic problems, I sanction with all my heart the obligation that rests on every patriotic citizen to make party second to country, and in the measure that he has been actuated by this broad and patriotic policy he will receive the plaudits of the whole people: "Well done, good and faithful servant."

Portentous indeed have been the developments of the past six months; the national domain has been extended far into the Caribbean Sea on the south, and to the west it is so near the mainland of Asia that we can hear grating of the process which is grinding the ancient celestial empire into pulp for the machinery of civilization and of progress.

But speaking as a Southerner and an American, I say that this has been as naught compared to the greatest good this war has accomplished. Drawing alike from all sections of the Union for her heroes and her martyrs, depending alike upon North, South, East and West for her glorious victories, and weeping with sympathy with the widows and the stricken mothers wherever they may be, America, incarnated spirit of liberty, stands again to-day the holy emblem of a household in which the children abide in unity, equality, love and peace. The iron sledge of war that rent asunder the links of loyalty and love has welded them together again. Ears that were deaf to loving appeals for the burial of sectional strife have listened and believed when the muster guns have spoken. Hearts that were cold to calls for trust and sympathy have awakened to loving confidence in the

[23] William McKinley.

baptism of their blood.

Drawing inspiration from the flag of our country, the South has shared not only the dangers, but the glories of the war. In the death of brave young Bagley at Cardenas, North Carolina furnished the first blood in the tragedy. It was Victor Blue of South Carolina, who, like the Swamp Fox of the Revolution, crossed the fiery path of the enemy at his pleasure, and brought the first official tidings of the situation as it existed in Cuba. It was Brumby, a Georgia boy, the flag lieutenant of Dewey, who first raised the stars and stripes over Manila. It was Alabama that furnished Hobson who accomplished two things the Spanish navy never yet has done—sunk an American ship, and made a Spanish man-of-war securely float.

The South answered the call to arms with its heart, and its heart goes out with that of the North in rejoicing at the result. The demonstration lacking to give the touch of life to the picture has been made. The open sesame that was needed to give insight into the true and loyal hearts both North and South has been spoken. Divided by war, we are united as never before by the same agency, and the union is of hearts as well as hands.

The doubter may scoff, and the pessimist may croak, but even they must take hope at the picture presented in the simple and touching incident of eight Grand Army veterans, with their silvery heads bowed in sympathy, escorting the lifeless body of the Daughter of the Confederacy from Narragansett to its last, long rest at Richmond.

When that great and generous soldier, U. S. Grant, gave back to Lee, crushed, but ever glorious, the sword he had surrendered at Appomattox, that magnanimous deed said to the people of the South: "You are our brothers." But when the present ruler of our grand republic on awakening to the condition of war that confronted him, with his first commission placed the leader's sword in the hands of those gallant confederate commanders, Joe Wheeler and Fitzhugh Lee, he wrote between the lines in living letters of everlasting light the words: "There is but one people of this Union, one flag alone for all."

The South, Mr. Toastmaster, will feel that her sons have been well given, that her blood has been well spilled, if that sentiment is to be indeed the true inspiration of our nation's future. God grant it may be as I believe it will.

# THE BLUE AND THE GRAY
## CLARK HOWELL

Speech of Henry Cabot Lodge, delivered at a banquet complimentary to the Robert E. Lee Camp of Confederate Veterans, of Richmond, Va., given in Faneuil Hall, Boston, June 17, 1887. The Southerners were visiting Boston as the special guests of the John A. Andrew Post 15, Department of Massachusetts, Grand Army of the Republic.

MR. CHAIRMAN:—To such a toast, sir, it would seem perhaps most fitting that one of those should respond who were a part of the great event which it recalls. Yet, after all, on an occasion like this, it may not be amiss to call upon one who belongs to a generation to whom the Rebellion is little more than history, and who, however insufficiently, represents the feelings of that and the succeeding generations as to our great Civil War. I was a boy ten years old when the troops marched away to defend Washington, and my personal knowledge of that time is confined to a few broken but vivid memories. I saw the troops, month after month, pour through the streets of Boston, I saw Shaw go forth at the head of his black regiment, and Bartlett, shattered in body but dauntless in soul, ride by to carry what was left of him once more to the battlefields of the republic. I saw Andrew, standing bare headed on the steps of the state house, bid the men God speed. I cannot remember the words he said, but I can never forget the fervid eloquence which brought tears to the eyes and fire to the hearts of all who listened. I understood but dimly the awful meaning of these events. To my boyish mind one thing alone was clear, that the soldiers as they marched past were all, in that supreme hour, heroes and patriots. Amid many changes that simple belief of boyhood has never altered. The gratitude which I felt then I confess to-day more strongly than ever. But other feelings have in the progress of time altered much. I have learned, and others of my generation as they came to man's estate have learned, what the war really meant, and they have also learned to know and to do justice to the men who fought the war upon the other side.

I do not stand up in this presence to indulge in any mock sentimentality. You brave men who wore the gray would be the first to hold me or any other son of the North in just contempt if I should say that, now it was all over, I thought the North was wrong and the result of the war a mistake, and that I was prepared to suppress my political opinions. I believe most profoundly that the war on our side was eternally right, that our victory was the salvation of the country, and that the results of the war were of infinite benefit to both North and South. But however we differed, or still differ, as to the causes for which we fought then, we accept them as settled, commit them to history, and fight over them no more. To the men who fought the battles of the Confederacy we hold out our hands freely, frankly, and gladly. To courage and faith wherever shown we bow in homage with uncovered heads. We respect and honor the gallantry and valor of the brave men who fought against us, and who gave their lives and shed their blood in defense of what they believed to be right. We rejoice that the famous general whose name is borne upon your banner was one of the greatest soldiers of modern times, because he, too, was an American. We have no bitter memories to revive, no reproaches to utter. Reconciliation is not to be sought, because it exists already. Differ in politics and in a thousand other ways we must and shall in all good nature, but let us never differ with each other on sectional or State lines, by race or creed.

We welcome you, soldiers of Virginia, as others more eloquent than I have said, to New England. We welcome you to old Massachusetts. We welcome you to Boston and to Faneuil Hall. In your presence here, and at the sound of your voices beneath this historic roof, the years roll back and we see the figure and hear again the ringing tones of your great orator, Patrick Henry, declaring to the first Continental Congress, "The distinctions between Virginians, Pennsylvanians, New Yorkers, and New Englanders are no more. I am not a Virginian, but an American." A distinguished Frenchman, as he stood among the graves at Arlington, said "Only a great people is capable of a great civil war." Let us add with thankful hearts that only a great people is capable of a great reconciliation. Side by side, Virginia and Massachusetts led the colonies into the War for Independence. Side by side they founded the government of the United States. Morgan and Greene, Lee and Knox, Moultrie and Prescott, men of the South and men of the North, fought shoulder to shoulder, and wore the same uniform of buff and blue—the uniform of Washington.

Your presence here brings back their noble memories, it breathes the spirit of concord, and united with so many other voices in the irrevocable message of union and good will. Mere sentiment all this, some may say. But it is sentiment, true sentiment, that has moved the world. Sentiment fought the war, and sentiment has reunited us. When the war closed, it was proposed in the newspapers and elsewhere to give Governor Andrew, who had sacrificed health and strength and property in his public duties, some immediately lucrative office, like the collectorship of the port of Boston. A friend asked him if he would take such a place. "No," said he; "I have stood as high priest between the horns of the altar, and I have poured out upon it the best blood of Massachusetts, and I cannot take money for that." Mere sentiment, truly, but the sentiment which ennobles and uplifts mankind. It is sentiment which so hallows a bit of torn, stained bunting, that men go gladly to their deaths to save it. So I say that the sentiment manifested by your presence here, brethren of Virginia, sitting side by side with those who wore the blue, has a far-reaching and gracious influence, of more value than many practical things. It tells us that these two grand old commonwealths, parted in the shock of the Civil War, are once more side by side as in the days of the Revolution, never to part again. It tells us that the sons of Virginia and Massachusetts, if war should break again upon the country, will, as in the olden days, stand once more shoulder to shoulder, with no distinction in the colors that they wear. It is fraught with tidings of peace on earth and you may read its meaning in the words on yonder picture, "Liberty and Union, now and forever, one and inseparable."

# A REMINISCENCE OF GETTYSBURG

## JOHN B. GORDON

The following extract is taken from General John B. Gordon's great lecture, "The Last Days of the Confederacy," delivered with marked effect throughout the country. This report of the lecture is as given in Brooklyn, N. Y., February 7, 1901.

But now to Gettysburg. That great battle could not be described in the space of a lecture. I shall select from the myriad of thrilling incidents which rush over my memory but two.[24] The first I relate because it seems due to one of the bravest and knightliest soldiers of the Union army. As my command came back from the Susquehanna River to Gettysburg, it was thrown squarely on the right flank of the Union army. The fact that that portion of the Union army melted was no disparagement either of its courage or its lofty American manhood, for any troops that had ever been marshaled, the Old Guard itself, would have been as surely and swiftly shattered. It was that movement that gave to the Confederate army the first day's victory at Gettysburg; and as I rode forward over that field of green clover, made red with the blood of both armies, I found a major-general among the dead and the dying. But a few moments before, I had seen the proud form of that magnificent Union officer reel in the saddle and then fall in the white smoke of the battle; and as I rode by, intensely looking into his pale face, which was turned to the broiling rays of that scorching July sun, I discovered that he was not dead. Dismounting from my horse, I lifted his head with one hand, gave him water from my canteen, inquired his name and if he was badly hurt. He was General Francis C. Barlow, of New York. He had been shot from his horse while grandly leading a charge. The ball had struck him in front, passed through the body and out near the spinal cord, completely paralyzing him in every limb; neither he nor I supposed he could live for one hour. I desired to remove him before death from that terrific sun. I had him lifted on a litter and borne to the shade in the rear. As he bade me good-bye, and upon my inquiry what I could do for him, he asked me to take from his pocket a bunch of letters. Those letters were from his wife, and as I opened one at his request, and as his eye caught, as he supposed for the last time, that wife's signature, the great tears came like a fountain and rolled down his pale face; and he said to me, "General Gordon, you are a Confederate; I am a Union soldier; but we are both Americans; if you should live through this dreadful war and ever see my wife, will you not do me the kindness to tell my wife for me that you saw me on this field? Tell her for me, that my last thought on earth was of her; tell her for

[24] But one of these incidents is given in this extract.

me that you saw me fall in this battle, and that her husband fell, not in the rear, but at the head of his column; tell her for me, general, that I freely give my life to my country, but that my unutterable grief is that I must now go without the privilege of seeing her once more, and bidding her a long and loving farewell." I at once said: "Where is Mrs. Barlow, general? Where could I find her?" for I was determined that wife should receive that gallant husband's message. He replied: "She is very close to me; she is just back of the Union line of battle with the commander-in-chief at his headquarters." That announcement of Mrs. Barlow's presence with the Union army struck in this heart of mine another chord of deepest and tenderest sympathy; for my wife had followed me, sharing with me the privations of the camp, the fatigues of the march; again and again was she under fire, and always on the very verge of the battle was that devoted wife of mine, like an angel of protection and an inspiration to duty. I replied: "Of course, General Barlow, if I am alive, sir, when this day's battle, now in progress is ended—if I am not shot dead before the night comes—you may die satisfied that I will see to it that Mrs. Barlow has your message before to-morrow's dawn."

And I did. The moment the guns had ceased their roar on the hills, I sent a flag of truce with a note to Mrs. Barlow. I did not tell her—I did not have the heart to tell her that her husband was dead, as I believed him to be; but I did tell her that he was desperately wounded, a prisoner in my hands; but that she should have safe escort through my lines to her husband's side. Late that night, as I lay in the open field upon my saddle, a picket from my front announced a lady on the line. She was Mrs. Barlow. She had received my note and was struggling, under the guidance of officers of the Union army, to penetrate my lines and reach her husband's side. She was guided to his side by my staff during the night. Early next morning the battle was renewed, and the following day, and then came the retreat of Lee's immortal army. I thought no more of that gallant son of the North, General Barlow, except to count him among the thousands of Americans who had gone down on both sides in the dreadful battle. Strangely enough, as the war progressed, Barlow concluded not to die; Providence decreed that he should live. He recovered and rejoined his command; and just one year after that, Barlow saw that I was killed in another battle. The explanation is perfectly simple. A cousin of mine, with the same initials, General J. B. Gordon, of North Carolina, was killed in a battle near Richmond. Barlow, who, as I say, had recovered and rejoined his command—although I knew he was dead, or thought I did—picked up a newspaper and read this item in it: "General J. B. Gordon of the Confederate army was killed to-day in battle." Calling his staff around him, Barlow read that item and said to them, "I am very sorry to see this; you will remember that General J. B. Gordon was the officer who picked me up on the battlefield at Gettysburg, and sent my wife through his lines to me at night. I am very sorry."

Fifteen years passed. Now, I wish the audience to remember that during all those fifteen years which intervened, Barlow was dead to me, and for fourteen of them I was dead to Barlow. In the meantime, the partiality of the people of Georgia had placed me in the United States senate. Clarkson Potter was a member of Congress from New York. He invited me to dine with him to meet his friend,

General Barlow. Now came my time to think. "Barlow," I said, "Barlow? That is the same name, but it can't be my Barlow, for I left him dead at Gettysburg." And I endeavored to understand what it meant, and thought I had made the discovery. I was told, as I made the inquiry, that there were two Barlows in the United States army. That satisfied me at once. I concluded, as a matter of course, that it was the other fellow I was going to meet; that Clarkson Potter had invited me to dine with the living Barlow and not with the dead one. Barlow had a similar reflection about the Gordon he was to dine with. He supposed that I was the other Gordon. We met at Clarkson Potter's table. I sat just opposite to Barlow; and in the lull of the conversation I asked him, "General, are you related to the Barlow who was killed at Gettysburg?" He replied: "I am the man, sir." "Are you related," he asked, "to the Gordon who killed me?" "Well," I said, "I am the man, sir." The scene which followed beggars all description. No language could describe that scene at Clarkson Potter's table in Washington, fifteen years after the war was over. Truth is indeed stranger than fiction. Think of it! What could be stranger? There we met, both dead, each of us presenting to the other the most absolute proof of the resurrection of the dead.

But stranger still, perhaps, is the friendship true and lasting begun under such auspices. What could be further removed from the realms of probabilities than a confiding friendship between combatants, which is born on the field of blood, amidst the thunders of battle, and while the hostile legions rush upon each other with deadly fury and pour into each other's breasts their volleys of fire and of leaden hail. Such were the circumstances under which was born the friendship between Barlow and myself, and which I believe is more sincere because of its remarkable birth, and which has strengthened and deepened with the passing years. For the sake of our reunited and glorious Republic may we not hope that similar ties will bind together all the soldiers of the two armies—indeed all Americans in perpetual unity until the last bugle call shall have summoned us to the eternal camping grounds beyond the stars?

# THE NEW SOUTH

## HENRY W. GRADY

Address by Henry W. Grady, journalist [born in Athens, Ga., May 17, 1851; died in Atlanta, Ga., December 23, 1889], delivered at the eighty-first anniversary celebration of the New England Society in the city of New York, December 22, 1886.

MR. PRESIDENT AND GENTLEMEN:—"There was a South of slavery and secession—that South is dead. There is a South of union and freedom—that South, thank God, is living, breathing, growing every hour." These words, delivered from the immortal lips of Benjamin H. Hill, at Tammany Hall in 1866, true then, and truer now, I shall make my text to-night.

Let me express to you my appreciation of the kindness by which I am permitted to address you. I make this abrupt acknowledgment advisedly, for I feel that if, when I raise my provincial voice in this ancient and august presence, I could find courage for no more than the opening sentence, it would be well if, in that sentence, I had met in a rough sense my obligation as a guest, and had perished, so to speak, with courtesy on my lips and grace in my heart. Permitted through your kindness to catch my second wind, let me say that I appreciate the significance of being the first Southerner to speak at this board, which bears the substance, if it surpasses the semblance, of original New England hospitality and honors a sentiment that in turn honors you, but in which my personality is lost, and the compliment to my people made plain.

I bespeak the utmost stretch of your courtesy to-night. I am not troubled about those from whom I come. You remember the man whose wife sent him to a neighbor with a pitcher of milk, and who, tripping on the top step, fell, with such casual interruptions as the landing afforded, into the basement; and while picking himself up had the pleasure of hearing his wife call out: "John, did you break the pitcher?" "No, I didn't," said John, "but I be dinged if I don't!"

So, while those who call to me from behind may inspire me with energy if not with courage, I ask an indulgent hearing from you. I beg that you will bring your full faith in American fairness and frankness to judgment upon what I shall say. There was an old preacher once who told some boys of the Bible lesson he was going to read in the morning. The boys finding the place, glued together the connecting pages. The next morning he read on the bottom of one page: "When Noah was one hundred and twenty years old he took unto himself a wife, who was"—then turning the page—"one hundred and forty cubits long, forty cubits wide, built of gopher wood, and covered with pitch inside and out." He was naturally puzzled at this. He read it again, verified it, and then said: "My friends, this is the first time I ever met this in the Bible, but I accept it as an evidence of the assertion that we are fearfully and wonderfully made." If I could get you to hold such faith to-night I could proceed cheerfully to the task I otherwise approach with a sense of consecration.

Pardon me one word, Mr. President, spoken for the sole purpose of getting into the volumes that go out annually freighted with the rich eloquence of your speakers—the fact that the Cavalier as well as the Puritan was on the continent in its early days, and that he was "up and able to be about." I have read your books carefully and I find no mention of that fact, which seems to me an important one for preserving a sort of historical equilibrium if for nothing else. Let me remind you the Virginia Cavalier first challenged France on this continent—that Cavalier John Smith gave New England its very name, and was so pleased with the job that he has been handing his own name around ever since—and that while Miles Standish was cutting off men's ears for courting a girl without her parents' consent, and forbade men to kiss their wives on Sunday, the Cavalier was courting everything in sight, and that the Almighty had vouchsafed great increase to the Cavalier colonies, the huts in the wilderness being full as the nests in the woods.

But having incorporated the Cavalier as a fact in your charming little books I shall let him work out his own salvation, as he has always done with engaging gallantry, and we will hold no controversy as to his merits. Why should we? Neither Puritan nor Cavalier long survived as such. The virtues and traditions of both happily still live for the inspiration of their sons and the saving of the old fashion. But both Puritan and Cavalier were lost in the storm of the first Revolution; and the American citizen, supplanting both and stronger than either, took possession of the Republic bought by their common blood and fashioned to wisdom, and charged himself with teaching men government and establishing the voice of the people as the voice of God.

My friend, Dr. Talmage has told you that the typical American has yet to come. Let me tell you that he has already come. Great types like valuable plants are slow to flower and fruit. But from the union of these colonies Puritans and Cavaliers, from the straightening of their purposes and the crossing of their blood, slow perfecting through a century, came he who stands as the first typical American, the first who comprehended within himself all the strength and gentleness, all the majesty and grace of this Republic—Abraham Lincoln. He was the son of Puritan and Cavalier, for in his ardent nature were fused the virtues of both, and in the depths of his great soul the faults of both were lost. He was greater than Puritan, greater than Cavalier, in that he was American renewed, and that in his homely form were first gathered the vast and thrilling forces of his ideal government—charging it with such tremendous meaning and so elevating it above human suffering that martyrdom, though infamously aimed, came as a fitting crown to a life consecrated from the cradle to human liberty. Let us, each cherishing the traditions and honoring his fathers, build with reverent hands to the type of this simple but sublime life, in which all types are honored; and in our common glory as Americans there will be plenty and to spare for your forefathers and for mine.

In speaking to the toast with which you have honored me. I accent the term, "The New South," as in no sense disparaging to the Old. Dear to me, sir, is the home of my childhood and the traditions of my people. I would not, if I could, dim the glory they won in peace and war, or by word or deed take aught from the splendor and grace of their civilization—never equaled and, perhaps, never to be equaled in its chivalric strength and grace. There is a New South, not through protest against the Old, but because of new conditions, new adjustments and, if you please, new ideas and aspirations. It is to this that I address myself, and to the consideration of which I hasten lest it become the Old South before I get to it. Age does not endow all things with strength and virtue, nor are all new things to be despised. The shoemaker who put over his door "John Smith's shop. Founded in 1760," was more than matched by his young rival across the street who hung out this sign: "Bill Jones. Established 1886. No old stock kept in this shop."

Dr. Talmage has drawn for you, with a master's hand, the picture of your returning armies. He has told you how, in the pomp and circumstance of war, they came back to you, marching with proud and victorious tread, reading their glory in a nation's eyes! Will you bear with me while I tell you of another army that sought its home at the close of the late war—an army that marched home in defeat and not in victory—in pathos and not in splendor, but in glory that equalled yours, and to hearts as loving as ever welcomed heroes home. Let me picture to you the footsore Confederate soldier, as, buttoning up in his faded gray jacket the parole which was to bear testimony to his children of his fidelity and faith, he turned his face southward from Appomattox in April, 1865. Think of him as ragged, half-starved, heavy-hearted, enfeebled by want and wounds; having fought to exhaustion, he surrenders his gun, wrings the hands of his comrades in silence, and lifting his tear-stained and pallid face for the last time to the graves that dot the old Virginia hills, pulls his gray cap over his brow and begins the slow and painful journey. What does he find—let me ask you, who went to your homes eager to find in the welcome you had justly earned, full payment for four years' sacrifice—what does he find when, having followed the battle-stained cross against overwhelming odds, dreading death not half so much as surrender, he reaches the home he left so prosperous and beautiful? He finds his house in ruins, his farm devastated, his slaves free, his stock killed, his barns empty, his trade destroyed, his money worthless; his social system, feudal in its magnificence, swept away; his people without law or legal status, his comrades slain, and the burdens of others heavy on his shoulders. Crushed by defeat, his very traditions are gone; without money, credit, employment, material or training; and besides all this, confronted with the gravest problem that ever met human intelligence—the establishing of a status for the vast body of his liberated slaves.

What does he do—this hero in gray with a heart of gold? Does he sit down in sullenness and despair? Not for a day. Surely God, who had stripped him of his prosperity, inspired him in his adversity. As ruin was never before so overwhelming, never was restoration swifter. The soldier stepped from the trenches into the furrow; horses that had charged Federal guns marched before the plow, and fields that ran red with human blood in April were green with the harvest in June; women reared in luxury cut up their dresses and made breeches for their husbands, and, with a patience and heroism that fit women always as a garment, gave their hands to work. There was little bitterness in all this. Cheerfulness and frankness prevailed. "Bill Arp" struck the keynote when he said: "Well, I killed as many of them as they did of me, and now I am going to work." Or the soldier returning home after defeat and roasting some corn on the roadside, who made the remark to his comrades: "You may leave the South if you want to, but I am going to Sandersville, kiss my wife and raise a crop, and if the Yankees fool with me any more I will whip 'em again." I want to say to General Sherman—who is considered an able man in our part, though some people think he is a kind of careless man about fire—that from the ashes he left us in 1864 we have raised a brave and beautiful city; that somehow or other we have caught the sunshine in the bricks and mortar of our homes, and have builded therein not one ignoble prejudice or memory.

But in all this what have we accomplished? What is the sum of our work? We have found out that in the general summary the free negro counts more than he did as a slave. We have planted the schoolhouse on the hilltop and made it free to white and black. We have sowed towns and cities in the place of theories and put business above politics. We have challenged your spinners in Massachusetts and your iron-makers in Pennsylvania. We have learned that the $400,000,000 annually received from our cotton crop will make us rich, when the supplies that make it are homeraised. We have reduced the commercial rate of interest from twenty-four to six per cent., and are floating four per cent. bonds. We have learned that one Northern immigrant is worth fifty foreigners, and have smoothed the path to southward, wiped out the place where Mason and Dixon's line used to be, and hung our latch-string out, to you and yours. We have reached the point that marks perfect harmony in every household, when the husband confesses that the pies which his wife cooks are as good as those his mother used to bake; and we admit that the sun shines as brightly and the moon as softly as it did "before the war." We have established thrift in city and country. We have fallen in love with work. We have restored comfort to homes from which culture and elegance never departed. We have let economy take root and spread among us as rank as the crabgrass which sprung from Sherman's cavalry camps, until we are ready to lay odds on the Georgia Yankee, as he manufactures relics of the battlefield in a one-story shanty and squeezes pure olive oil out of his cotton seed, against any down-easter that ever swapped wooden nutmegs for flannel sausages in the valleys of Vermont. Above all, we know that we have achieved in these "piping times of peace" a fuller independence for the South than that which our fathers sought to win in the forum by their eloquence or compel on the field by their swords.

It is a rare privilege, sir, to have had part, however humble, in this work. Never was nobler duty confided to human hands than the uplifting and upbuilding of the prostrate and bleeding South, misguided, perhaps, but beautiful in her suffering, and honest, brave and generous always. In the record of her social, industrial, and political institutions we await with confidence the verdict of the world.

But what of the negro? Have we solved the problem he presents or progressed in honor and equity towards the solution? Let the record speak to the point. No section shows a more prosperous laboring population than the negroes of the South; none in fuller sympathy with the employing and landowning class. He shares our school fund, has the fullest protection of our laws and the friendship of our people. Self-interest, as well as honor, demand that he should have this. Our future, our very existence depend upon our working out this problem in full and exact justice. We understand that when Lincoln signed the Emancipation Proclamation, your victory was assured; for he then committed you to the cause of human liberty, against which the arms of man cannot prevail; while those of our statesmen who trusted to make slavery the cornerstone of the Confederacy doomed us to defeat as far as they could, committing us to a cause that reason could not defend or the sword maintain in the sight of advancing civilization. Had Mr. Toombs said, which he did not say, that he would call the roll of his slaves at the foot of Bunker Hill, he would have been foolish, for he might have known that whenever slavery became entangled in war it must perish, and that the chattel in human flesh ended forever in New England when your fathers—not to be blamed for parting with what didn't pay—sold their slaves to our fathers—not to be praised for knowing a paying thing when they saw it.

The relations of the Southern people with the negro are close and cordial. We remember with what fidelity for four years he guarded our defenseless women and children, whose husbands and fathers were fighting against his freedom. To his eternal credit be it said that whenever he struck a blow for his own liberty he fought in open battle, and when at last he raised his black and humble hands that the shackles might be struck off, those hands were innocent of wrong against his helpless charges, and worthy to be taken in loving grasp by every man who honors loyalty and devotion. Ruffians have maltreated him, rascals have misled him, philanthropists established a bank for him, but the South, with the North, protests against injustice to this simple and sincere people. To liberty and enfranchisement is as far as law can carry the negro. The rest must be left to conscience and common sense. It should be left to those among whom his lot is cast, with whom he is indissolubly connected and whose prosperity depends upon their possessing his intelligent sympathy and confidence. Faith has been kept with him in spite of calumnious assertions to the contrary by those who assume to speak for us or by frank opponents. Faith will be kept with him in the future, if the South holds her reason and integrity.

But have we kept faith with you? In the fullest sense, yes. When Lee surrendered—I don't say when Johnston surrendered, because I understand he still alludes to the time when he met General Sherman last as the time when he "determined to abandon any further prosecution of the struggle"—when Lee surrendered, I say, and Johnston quit, the South became, and has since been, loyal to this Union. We fought hard enough to know that we were whipped, and in perfect frankness accepted as final the arbitrament of the sword to which we had appealed. The South found her jewel in the toad's head of defeat. The shackles that had held her in narrow limitations fell forever when the shackles of the negro slave were broken. Under the old *regime* the negroes were slaves to the South, the South was a slave to the system. The old plantation, with its simple police regulation and its feudal habit, was the only type possible under slavery. Thus we gathered in the hands of a splendid and chivalric oligarchy the substance that should have been diffused among the people, as the rich blood, under certain artificial conditions, is gathered at the heart, filling with affluent rapture, but leaving the body chill and colorless.

The Old South rested everything on slavery and agriculture, unconscious that these could neither give nor maintain healthy growth. The New South presents a perfect democracy, the oligarchs leading in the popular movement—a social system compact and closely knitted, less splendid on the surface but stronger at the core—a hundred farms for every plantation, fifty homes for every palace, and diversified industry that meets the complex needs of this complex age.

The New South is enamored of her new work. Her soul is stirred with the breath of a new life. The light of a grander day is falling fair on her face. She is thrilling with the consciousness of growing power and prosperity. As she stands upright, full-statured and equal among the people of the earth, breathing the keen air and looking out upon the expanding horizon, she understands that her emancipation came because in the inscrutable wisdom of God her honest purpose was crossed and her brave armies were beaten.

This is said in no spirit of time-serving or apology. The South has nothing for which to apologize. She believes that the late struggle between the states was war and not rebellion, revolution and not conspiracy, and that her convictions were as honest as yours. I should be unjust to the dauntless spirit of the South and to my own convictions if I did not make this plain in this presence. The South has nothing to take back. In my native town of Athens is a monument that crowns its central hills—a plain, white shaft. Deep cut into its shining side is a name dear to me above the names of men, that of a brave and simple man who died in brave and simple faith. Not for all the glories of New England—from Plymouth Rock all the way—would I exchange the heritage he left me in his soldier's death. To the foot of that shaft I shall send my children's children to reverence him who ennobled their name with his heroic blood. But, sir, speaking from the shadow of that memory, which I honor as I do nothing else on earth, I say that the cause in which he suffered and for which he gave his life was adjudged by higher and fuller wisdom than his or mine, and I am glad that the omniscient God held the balance of battle in His Almighty hand, and that human slavery was swept forever from American soil—the American Union saved from the wreck of war.

This message, Mr. President, comes to you from consecrated ground. Every foot of the soil about the city in which I live is sacred as a battleground of the Republic. Every hill that invests it is hallowed to you by the blood of your brothers, who died for your victory, and doubly hallowed to us by the blood of those who died hopeless, but undaunted, in defeat—sacred soil to all of us, rich with memories that make us purer and stronger and better, silent but stanch witnesses in its red desolation of the matchless valor of American hearts and the deathless glory of American arms—speaking in eloquent witness in its white peace and prosperity to the indissoluble union of American states and the imperishable brotherhood of the American people.

Now, what answer has New England to this message? Will she permit the prejudices of war to remain in the hearts of the conquerors, when it has died in the hearts of the conquered? ("No! No!") Will she transmit this prejudice to the next generation, that in their hearts, which never felt the generous ardor of conflict, it may perpetuate itself? ("No! No!") Will she withhold, save in strained courtesy, the hand which straight from his soldier's heart Grant offered to Lee at Appomattox? Will she make the vision of a restored and happy people, which gathered above the couch of your dying captain, filling his heart with grace, touching his lips with praise and glorifying his path to the grave; will she make this vision on which the last sigh of his expiring soul breathed a benediction, a cheat and a delusion? If she does, the South, never abject in asking for comradeship, must accept with dignity its refusal; but if she does not; if she accepts in frankness and sincerity this message of goodwill and friendship, then will the prophecy of Webster, delivered in this very Society forty years ago amid tremendous applause, be verified in its fullest and final sense, when he said: "Standing hand to hand and clasping hands, we should remain united as we have been for sixty years, citizens of the same country, members of the same government, united, all united now and united forever. There have been difficulties, contentions, and controversies, but I tell you that in my judgment

> "'Those opposed eyes,
> Which like the meteors of a troubled heaven,
> All of one nature, of one substance bred,
> Did lately meet in th' intestine shock,
> Shall now, in mutual well-beseeming ranks,
> March all one way.'"

# THE DUTY AND VALUE OF PATRIOTISM
## ARCHBISHOP IRELAND

John Ireland, Archbishop of Saint Paul, was born at Burnchurch, County Kilkenny, Ireland, September 11, 1838. As a boy he came to Saint Paul, Minnesota, in 1849, and there obtained his secular education at the Cathedral School. He studied theology in France, in the seminaries of Meximieux and Hyeres. During the Civil War he was chaplain of the Fifth Minnesota Regiment. In 1875 he was consecrated bishop of Saint Paul. In 1869 he founded the first total-abstinence society in Minnesota and has lectured much on temperance in the United States and Great Britain. The following extracts, used by special permission, are from his lecture delivered before the New York Commandery of the Loyal Legion, New York, April 4, 1894.

Patriotism is love of country, and loyalty to its life and weal—love tender and strong, tender as the love of son for mother, strong as the pillars of death; loyalty generous and disinterested, shrinking from no sacrifice, seeking no reward save country's honor and country's triumph.

Patriotism! There is magic in the word. It is bliss to repeat it. Through ages the human race burnt the incense of admiration and reverence at the shrines of patriotism. The most beautiful pages of history are those which recount its deeds. Fireside tales, the outpourings of the memories of peoples, borrow from it their warmest glow. Poets are sweetest when they reecho its whisperings; orators are most potent when they thrill its chords to music.

Pagan nations were wrong when they made gods of their noblest patriots. But the error was the excess of a great truth, that heaven unites with earth in approving and blessing patriotism; that patriotism is one of earth's highest virtues, worthy to have come down from the atmosphere of the skies.

The exalted patriotism of the exiled Hebrew exhaled itself in a canticle of religion which Jehovah inspired, and which has been transmitted, as the inheritance of God's people to the Christian Church:

> "Upon the rivers of Babylon there we sat and wept, when we remembered Sion.—If I forget thee, O Jerusalem, let my right hand be forgotten. Let my tongue cleave to my jaws, if I do not remember thee, if I do not make Jerusalem the beginning of my joy."

The human race pays homage to patriotism because of its supreme value. The value of patriotism to a people is above gold and precious stones, above commerce and industry, above citadels and warships. Patriotism is the vital spark of national honor; it is the fount of the nation's prosperity, the shield of the nation's safety. Take patriotism away, the nation's soul has fled, bloom and beauty have vanished from the nation's countenance.

The human race pays homage to patriotism because of its supreme loveliness. Patriotism goes out to what is among earth's possessions the most precious, the first and best and dearest—country—and its effusion is the fragrant flowering of the purest and noblest sentiments of the heart.

Patriotism is innate in all men; the absence of it betokens a perversion of human nature; but it grows its full growth only where thoughts are elevated and heart-beatings are generous.

Next to God is country, and next to religion is patriotism. No praise goes beyond its deserts. It is sublime in its heroic oblation upon the field of battle. "Oh glorious is he," exclaims in Homer the Trojan warrior, "who for his country falls!" It is sublime in the oft-repeated toil of dutiful citizenship. "Of all human doings," writes Cicero, "none is more honorable and more estimable than to merit well of the commonwealth."

Countries are of divine appointment. The Most High "divided the nations, separated the sons of Adam, and appointed the bounds of peoples." The physical and moral necessities of God's creatures are revelations of his will and laws. Man is born a social being. A condition of his existence and of his growth of mature age is the family. Nor does the family suffice to itself. A larger social organism is needed, into which families gather, so as to obtain from one another security to life and property and aid in the development of the faculties and powers with which nature has endowed the children of men.

The whole human race is too extensive and too diversified in interests to serve those ends: hence its subdivisions into countries or peoples. Countries have their providential limits—the waters of a sea, a mountain range, the lines of similarity of requirements or of methods of living. The limits widen in space according to the measure of the destinies which the great Ruler allots to peoples, and the importance of their parts in the mighty work of the cycles of years, the ever-advancing tide of humanity's evolution.

The Lord is the God of nations because he is the God of men. No nation is born into life or vanishes back into nothingness without his bidding. I believe in the providence of God over countries as I believe in his wisdom and his love, and my patriotism to my country rises within my soul invested with the halo of my religion to my God.

More than a century ago a trans-Atlantic poet and philosopher, reading well the signs, wrote:

> "Westward the course of empire takes its way.
> The first four acts already past,

> A fifth shall close the drama with the day;
> Time's noblest offspring is the last."

Berkeley's prophetic eye had descried America. What shall I say, in a brief discourse of my country's value and beauty, of her claims to my love and loyalty? I will pass by in silence her fields and forests, her rivers and seas, the boundless riches hidden beneath her soil and amid the rocks of her mountains, her pure and health-giving air, her transcendent wealth of nature's fairest and most precious gifts. I will not speak of the noble qualities and robust deeds of her sons, skilled in commerce and industry, valorous in war, prosperous in peace. In all these things America is opulent and great: but beyond them and above them in her singular grandeur, to which her material splendor is only the fitting circumstance.

America born into the family of nations in these latter times is the highest billow in humanity's evolution, the crowning effort of ages in the aggrandizement of man. Unless we take her in this altitude, we do not comprehend her; we belittle her towering stature and conceal the singular design of Providence in her creation.

America is the country of human dignity and human liberty.

When the fathers of the republic declared "that all men are created equal; that they are endowed by their Creator with certain inalienable rights; that among these are life, liberty, and the pursuit of happiness," a cardinal principle was enunciated which in its truth was as old as the race, but in practical realization almost unknown.

Slowly, amid sufferings and revolutions, humanity had been reaching out toward a reign of the rights of man. Ante-Christian paganism had utterly denied such rights. It allowed nothing to man as man; he was what wealth, place, or power made him. Even the wise Aristotle taught that some men were intended by nature to be slaves and chattels. The sweet religion of Christ proclaimed aloud the doctrine of the common fatherhood of God and the universal brotherhood of men.

Eighteen hundred years, however, went by, and the civilized world had not yet put its civil and political institutions in accord with its spiritual faith. The Christian Church was all this time leavening human society and patiently awaiting the promised fermentation. This came at last, and it came in America. It came in a first manifestation through the Declaration of Independence; it came in a second and final manifestation through President Lincoln's Proclamation of Emancipation.

In America all men are civilly and politically equal; all have the same rights; all wield the same arm of defense and of conquest, the suffrage; and the sole condition of rights and of power is simple manhood.

Liberty is the exemption from all restraint save that of the laws of justice and order; the exemption from submission to other men, except as they represent and enforce those laws. The divine gift of liberty to man is God's recognition of his greatness and his dignity. The sweetness of man's life and the power of growth lie in liberty. The loss of liberty is the loss of light and sunshine, the loss of life's best portion. Humanity, under the spell of heavenly memories, never ceased to dream of liberty and to aspire to its possession. Now and then, here and there, its refreshing breezes caressed humanity's brow. But not until the republic of the West was born, not until the Star-Spangled Banner rose toward the skies, was liberty caught up in humanity's embrace and embodied in a great and abiding nation.

In America the government takes from the liberty of the citizen only so much as is necessary for the weal of the nation, which the citizen by his own act freely concedes. In America there are no masters, who govern in their own rights, for their own interests, or at their own will. We have over us no Louis XIV, saying: "L'etat, c'est moi;" no Hohenzollern, announcing that in his acts as sovereign he is responsible only to his conscience and to God.

Ours is the government of the people, by the people, for the people. The government is our organized will. There is no state above or apart from the people. Rights begin with and go upward from the people. In other countries, even those apparently the most free, rights begin with and come downward from the state; the rights of citizens, the rights of the people, are concessions which have been painfully wrenched from the governing powers.

With Americans, whenever the organized government does not prove its grant, the liberty of the individual citizen is sacred and inviolable. Elsewhere there are governments called republics; universal suffrage constitutes the state; but, once constituted, the state is tyrannous and arbitrary, invades at will private rights, and curtails at will individual liberty. One republic is liberty's native home—America.

# OUR COUNTRY

## WILLIAM MCKINLEY

From the speech of President McKinley, in response to the toast
"Our Country," at the Peace Jubilee banquet in Chicago, October
19, 1898.

Mr. Toastmaster and Gentlemen:—It affords me gratification to meet the people of the city of Chicago and to participate with them in this patriotic celebration. Upon the suspension of hostilities of a foreign war, the first in our history for over half a century, we have met in a spirit of peace, profoundly grateful for the glorious advancement already made, and earnestly wishing in the final termination to realize an equally glorious fulfillment. With no feeling of exultation, but with profound thankfulness, we contemplate the events of the past five months. They have been too serious to admit of boasting or vain-glorification. They have been so full of responsibilities, immediate and prospective, as to admonish the soberest judgment and counsel the most conservative action.

This is not the time to fire the imagination, but rather to discover, in calm reason, the way to truth, and justice, and right, and when discovered to follow it with fidelity and courage, without fear, hesitation, or weakness.

The war has put upon the nation grave responsibilities. Their extent was not anticipated and could not have been well foreseen. We cannot escape the obligations of victory. We cannot avoid the serious questions which have been brought home to us by the achievements of our arms on land and sea. We are bound in conscience to keep and perform the covenants which the war has sacredly sealed with mankind. Accepting war for humanity's sake, we must accept all obligations which the war in duty and honor imposed upon us. The splendid victories we have achieved would be our eternal shame and not our everlasting glory if they led to the weakening of our original lofty purpose or to the desertion of the immortal principles on which the national government was founded, and in accordance with whose ennobling spirit it has ever since been faithfully administered.

The war with Spain was undertaken not that the United States should increase its territory, but that oppression at our very doors should be stopped. This noble sentiment must continue to animate us, and we must give to the world the full demonstration of the sincerity of our purpose. Duty determines destiny. Destiny which results from duty performed may bring anxiety and perils, but never failure and dishonor. Pursuing duty may not always lead by smooth paths. Another course may look easier and more attractive, but pursuing duty for duty's sake is always sure and safe and honorable. It is not within the power of man to foretell the future and to solve unerringly its mighty problems. Almighty God has His plans and methods for human progress, and not infrequently they are shrouded for the time being in impenetrable mystery. Looking backward we can see how the hand of destiny builded for us and assigned us tasks whose full meaning was not apprehended even by the wisest statesmen of their times.

Our colonial ancestors did not enter upon their war originally for independence. Abraham Lincoln did not start out to free the slaves, but to save the Union. The war with Spain was not of our seeking, and some of its consequences may not be to our liking. Our vision is often defective. Short-sightedness is a common malady, but the closer we get to things or they get to us the clearer our view and the less obscure our duty. Patriotism must be faithful as well as fervent; statesmanship must be wise as well as fearless—not the statesmanship which will command the applause of the hour, but the approving judgment of posterity.

The progress of a nation can alone prevent degeneration. There must be new life and purpose, or there will be weakness and decay. There must be broadening of thought as well as broadening of trade. Territorial expansion is not alone and always necessary to national advancement. There must be a constant movement toward a higher and nobler civilization, a civilization that shall make its conquests without resort to war and achieve its greatest victories pursuing the arts of peace.

In our present situation duty—and duty alone—should prescribe the boundary of our responsibilities and the scope of our undertakings. The final determination of our purposes awaits the action of the eminent men who are charged by the executive with the making of the treaty of peace, and that of the senate of the United States, which, by our constitution, must ratify and confirm it. We all hope and pray that the confirmation of peace will be as just and humane as the conduct and consummation of the war. When the work of the treaty-makers is done the work of the law-makers will begin. The one will settle the extent of our responsibilities; the other must provide the legislation to meet them. The army and navy have nobly and heroically performed their part. May God give the executive and congress wisdom to perform theirs.

# BEHOLD THE AMERICAN
## WILLIAM MCKINLEY

From the speech of Rev. Dr. T. DeWitt Talmage at the eighty-first annual dinner of the New England Society in New York, December 22, 1886.

MR. PRESIDENT, AND ALL YOU GOOD NEW ENGLANDERS:—If we leave to the evolutionists to guess where we came from and to the theologians to prophesy where are we going to, we still have left for consideration the fact that we are here; and we are here at an interesting time. Of all the centuries this is the best century, and of all the decades of the century this is the best decade, and of all the years of the decade this is the best year, and of all the months of the year this is the best month, and of all the nights of the month this is the best night. Many of these advantages we trace straight back to Forefathers' Day, about which I am to speak.

Well, what about this Forefathers' Day? In Brooklyn they say the Landing of the Pilgrims was December the 21st; in New York you say it was December the 22d. You are both right. Not through the specious and artful reasoning you have sometimes indulged in, but by a little historical incident that seems to have escaped your attention. You see, the Forefathers landed in the morning of December the 21st, but about noon that day a pack of hungry wolves swept down the bleak American beach looking for a New England dinner, and a band of savages out for a tomahawk picnic hove in sight, and the Pilgrim Fathers thought it best for safety and warmth to go on board the Mayflower and pass the night. And during the night there came up a strong wind blowing off shore that swept the Mayflower from its moorings clear out to sea, and there was a prospect that our Forefathers, having escaped oppression in foreign lands, would yet go down under an oceanic tempest. But the next day they fortunately got control of their ship and steered her in, and the second time the Forefathers stepped ashore.

Brooklyn celebrated the first landing; New York the second landing. So I say Hail! Hail! to both celebrations, for one day, anyhow, could not do justice to such a subject; and I only wish I could have kissed the Blarney stone of America, which is Plymouth Rock, so that I might have done justice to this subject. Ah, gentlemen, that Mayflower was the ark that floated the deluge of oppression, and Plymouth Rock was the Ararat on which it landed.

But all these things aside, no one sitting at these tables has higher admiration for the Pilgrim Fathers than I have—the men who believed in two great doctrines, which are the foundation of every religion that is worth anything: namely, the fatherhood of God and the brotherhood of Man—these men of backbone and endowed with that great and magnificent attribute of stick-to-it-iveness. Macaulay said that no one ever sneered at the Puritans who had met them in halls of debate or crossed swords with them on the field of battle. They are sometimes defamed for their rigorous Sabbaths, but our danger is in the opposite direction of no Sabbaths at all. It is said that they destroyed witches. I wish that they had cleared them all out, for all the world is full of witches yet, and if at all these tables there is a man who has not sometimes been bewitched, let him hold up his glass of ice-water. It is said that these Forefathers carried religion into everything, and before a man kissed his wife he asked a blessing, and afterward said: "Having received another favor from the Lord, let us return thanks." But our great need now is more religion in every-day life.

Still, take it all in all, I think the descendants of the Pilgrim Fathers are as good as their ancestors, and in many ways better. Children are apt to be an echo of their ancestors. We are apt to put a halo around the Forefathers, but I suspect that at our age they were very much like ourselves. People are not wise when they long for the good old days.

But though your Forefathers may not have been much, if any, better than yourselves, let us extol them for the fact that they started this country in the right direction. They laid the foundation for American manhood. The foundation must be more solid and firm and unyielding than any other part of the structure. On that Puritanic foundation we can safely build all nationalities. Let us remember that the coming American is to be an admixture of all foreign bloods. In about twenty-five or fifty years the model American will step forth. He will have the strong brain of the German, the polished manners of the French, the artistic taste of the Italian, the stanch heart of the English, the steadfast piety of the Scotch, the lightning wit of the Irish, and when he steps forth, bone, muscle, nerve, brain entwined with the fibers of all nationalities, the nations will break out in the cry: "Behold the American!"

I never realized what this country was and is as on the day when I first saw some of these gentlemen of the Army and Navy. It was when at the close of the War our armies came back and marched in review before the president's stand at Washington. I do not care whether a man was a Republican or a Democrat, a Northern man or a Southern man, if he had any emotion of nature, he could not look upon it without weeping. God knew that the day was stupendous, and He cleared the heaven of cloud and mist and chill, and sprung the blue sky as the triumphal arch for the returning warriors to pass under. From Arlington Heights the spring foliage shook out its welcome, as the hosts came over the hills, and the sparkling waters of the Potomac tossed their gold to the feet of the battalions as they came to the Long Bridge and in almost interminable line passed over. The capitol never seemed so majestic as that morning: snowy white, looking down upon the tides of men that came surging down, billow after billow. Passing in silence, yet I heard in every step the thunder of conflicts through which they had waded, and seemed to see dripping from their smoke-blackened flags the blood of our country's martyrs. For the best part of two days we stood and watched the filing on of what seemed endless battalions, brigade after brigade, division after division, host after host, rank beyond rank; ever moving, ever passing; marching, marching; tramp, tramp, tramp—thousands after thousands, battery front, arms shouldered, columns solid, shoulder to shoulder, wheel to wheel, charger to charger, nostril to nostril.

Commanders on horses with their manes entwined with roses, and necks enchained with garlands, fractious at the shouts that ran along the line, increasing from the clapping of children clothed in white, standing on the steps of the capitol, to the tumultuous vociferation of hundreds of thousands of enraptured multitudes, crying "Huzza! Huzza!" Gleaming muskets, thundering parks of artillery, rumbling pontoon wagons, ambulances from whose wheels seemed to sound out the groans of the crushed and the dying that they had carried. These men came from balmy Minnesota, those from Illinois prairies. These were often hummed to sleep by the pines of Oregon, those were New England lumbermen. Those came out of the coal-shafts of Pennsylvania. Side by side in one great cause, consecrated through fire and storm and darkness, brothers in peril, on their way home from Chancellorsville and Kenesaw Mountain and Fredericksburg, in lines that seemed infinite they passed on.

We gazed and wept and wondered, lifting up our heads to see if the end had come, but no! Looking from one end of that long avenue to the other, we saw them yet in solid column, battery front, host beyond host, wheel to wheel, charger to charger, nostril to nostril, coming as it were from under the capitol. Forward! Forward! Their bayonets, caught in the sun, glimmered and flashed and blazed, till they seemed like one long river of silver, ever and anon changed into a river of fire. No end to the procession, no rest for the eyes. We turned our heads from the scene, unable longer to look. We felt disposed to stop our ears, but still we heard it, marching, marching; tramp, tramp, tramp. But hush—uncover every head! Here they pass, the remnant of ten men of a full regiment. Silence! Widowhood and orphanage look on and wring their hands. But wheel into line, all ye people! North, South, East, West—all decades, all centuries, all millenniums! Forward, the whole line! Huzza! Huzza!

# THE HOLLANDER AS AN AMERICAN
## THEODORE ROOSEVELT

Speech of Theodore Roosevelt at the eleventh annual dinner of
the Holland Society of New York, January 15, 1896.

Mr. President, Gentlemen, and Brethren of the Holland Society:—I am
more than touched, if you will permit me to begin rather seriously, by the way
you have greeted me to-night. When I was in Washington, there was a story in
reference to a certain president, who was not popular with some of his own people
in a particular western state. One of its senators went to the White House and said
he wanted a friend of his appointed postmaster of Topeka. The president's private
secretary said, "I am very sorry, indeed, sir, but the president wants to appoint a
personal friend." Thereupon the senator said: "Well, for God's sake, if he has one
friend in Kansas, let him appoint him!"

There have been periods during which the dissembled eulogies of the able
press and my relations with about every politician of every party and every faction
have made me feel I would like to know whether I had one friend in New York,
and here I feel I have many. And more than that, gentlemen, I should think ill of
myself and think that I was a discredit to the stock from which I sprang if I feared
to go on along the path that I deemed right, whether I had few friends or many.

I am glad to answer to the toast, "The Hollander as an American." The Hollander was a good American, because the Hollander was fitted to be a good citizen.
There are two branches of government which must be kept on a high plane, if any
nation is to be great. A nation must have laws that are honestly and fearlessly administered, and it must be ready, in time of need, to fight; and we men of Dutch
descent have here to-night these gentlemen of the same blood as ourselves who
represent New York so worthily on the bench, and a major-general of the army of
the United States.

It seems to me, at times, that the Dutch in America have one or two lessons
to teach. We want to teach the very refined and very cultivated men who believe
it impossible that the United States can ever be right in a quarrel with another
nation—a little of the elementary virtue of patriotism. And we also wish to teach
our fellow citizens that laws are put on the statute books to be enforced and that if
it is not intended they shall be enforced it is a mistake to put a Dutchman in office
to enforce them.

The lines put on the program underneath my toast begin: "America! half
brother of the world!" America, half brother of the world—and all Americans full

brothers one to the other. That is the way that line should be concluded. The prime virtue of the Hollander here in America and the way in which he has most done credit to his stock as a Hollander, is that he has ceased to be a Hollander and has become an American, absolutely. We are not Dutch-Americans. We are not "Americans" with a hyphen before it. We are Americans pure and simple, and we have a right to demand that the other people whose stocks go to compose our great nation, like ourselves, shall cease to be aught else and shall become Americans.

And further than that, we have another thing to demand, and that is that if they do honestly and in good faith become Americans, those shall be regarded as infamous who dare to discriminate against them because of creed or because of birthplace. When New Amsterdam had but a few hundred souls, among those few hundred souls no less than eighteen different race stocks were represented, and almost as many creeds as there were race stocks, and the great contribution that the Hollander gave to the American people was the inestimable lesson of complete civil and religious liberty. It would be honor enough for this stock to have been the first to put on American soil the public school, the great engine for grinding out American citizens, the one institution for which Americans should stand more stiffly than for aught other.

Whenever America has demanded of her sons that they should come to her aid, whether in time of peace or in time of war, the Americans of Dutch stock have been among the first to spring to the aid of the country. We earnestly hope that there will not in the future be any war with any power, but assuredly if there should be such a war one thing may be taken for certain, and that is that every American of Dutch descent will be found on the side of the United States. We give the amplest credit, that some people now, to their shame, grudge to the profession of arms, which we have here to-night represented by a man, who, when he has the title of a major general of the army of the United States, has a title as honorable as any that there is on the wide earth. We also need to teach the lesson, that the Hollander taught, of not refusing to do the small things because the day of large things had not yet come or was in the past; of not waiting until the chance may come to distinguish ourselves in arms, and meanwhile neglecting the plain, prosaic duties of citizenship which call upon us every hour, every day of our lives.

The Dutch kept their freedom in the great contest with Spain, not merely because they warred valiantly, but because they did their duty as burghers in their cities, because they strove according to the light that was in them to be good citizens and to act as such. And we all here to-night should strive so to live that we Americans of Dutch descent shall not seem to have shrunk in this respect, compared to our fathers who spoke another tongue and lived under other laws beyond the ocean; so that it shall be acknowledged in the end to be what it is, a discredit to a man if he does not in times of peace do all that in him lies to make the government of the city, the government of the country, better and cleaner by his efforts.

I spoke of the militant spirit as if it may only be shown in time of war. I think that if any of you gentlemen, no matter how peaceful you may naturally be, and I am very peaceful naturally, if you would undertake the administration of the Police Department you would have plenty of fighting on hand before you would get through; and if you are true to your blood you will try to do the best you can, fighting or not fighting. You will make up your mind that you will make mistakes, because you won't make anything if you don't make some mistakes, and you will go forward according to your lights, utterly heedless of what either politicians or newspapers may say, knowing that if you act as you feel bound according to your conscience to act, you will then at least have the right when you go out of office, however soon, to feel that you go out without any regret, and to feel that you have according to your capacity, warred valiantly for what you deemed to be the right.

These, then, are the qualities that I should claim for the Hollander as an American: In the first place, that he has cast himself without reservation into the current of American life; that he is an American, pure and simple, and nothing else. In the next place, that he works hand in hand and shoulder to shoulder with his fellow Americans, without any regard to differences of creed or to differences of race and religion, if only they are good Americans. In the third place, that he is willing, when the need shall arise, to fight for his country; and in the fourth place, and finally, that he recognizes that this is a country of laws and not men, that it is his duty as an honest citizen to uphold the laws, to strive for honesty, to strive for a decent administration, and to do all that in him lies, by incessant, patient work in our government, municipal or national, to bring about the day when it shall be taken as a matter of course that every public official is to execute a law honestly, and that no capacity in a public officer shall atone if he is personally dishonest.

# THE ADOPTED CITIZEN
## THEODORE ROOSEVELT

Speech of Gen. Ulysses S. Grant at the 115th annual banquet of
the Chamber of Commerce of the State of New York, May 8, 1883.

MR. PRESIDENT AND GENTLEMEN OF THE CHAMBER OF COMMERCE AND GUESTS:—I
am very much obliged to your president for calling upon me first, because the agony will soon be over and I shall enjoy the misery of the rest of you.

The first part of this toast—The United States—would be a voluminous one
to respond to on a single occasion. Bancroft commenced to publish his notes on
the History of the United States, starting even before President Lane established
this Chamber, which I think was something over one hundred years ago. Bancroft, I say, commenced earlier, and I am not prepared to dispute his word if he
should say that he had kept an accurate journal from the time he commenced to
write about the country to the present, because there has been no period of time
when I have been alive that I have not heard of Bancroft, and I should be equally
credulous if President Lane should tell me that he was here at the founding of this
Institution. But instead of bringing those volumes of Bancroft's here, and reading
them to you on this occasion, I will let the reporters publish them as the prelude
to what I am going to say.

I think Bancroft has finished up to a little after the time that President Lane
established this Chamber of Commerce, and I will let you take the records of what
he (Lane) has written and what he has said in their monthly meetings and publish
them as the second chapter of my speech. And, gentlemen, those two chapters you
will find the longest; they will not amount to much more than what I have to say
taking up the subject at the present time.

But in speaking of the United States, we who are native-born have a country
of which we may well be proud. Those of us who have been abroad are better able,
perhaps, to make the comparison of our enjoyments and our comforts than those
who have always stayed at home. It has been the fortune, I presume, of the majority here to compare the life and the circumstances of the average people abroad
with ours here. We have here a country that affords room for all and room for every enterprise. We have institutions which encourage every man who has industry
and ability to rise from the position in which he may find himself to any position
in the land. It is hardly worth my while to dwell upon the subject, but there is one
point which I notice in the toast, that I would like to say a word about—*"May those
who seek the blessings of its free institutions and the protection of its flag remember the*

*obligations they impose."* I think there is a text that my friend Mr. Beecher,[25] on the left, or my friend Dr. Newman,[26] on the right, might well preach a long sermon upon. I shall say only a few words.

We offer an asylum to every man of foreign birth who chooses to come here and settle upon our soil; we make of him, after a few years' residence only, a citizen endowed with all the rights that any of us have, except perhaps the single one of being elected to the presidency of the United States. There is no other privilege that a native, no matter what he has done for the country, has that the adopted citizen of five years' standing has not got. I contend that that places upon him an obligation which, I am sorry to say, many of them do not seem to feel.

We have witnessed on many occasions here the foreign, the adopted, citizen claiming many rights and privileges because he was an adopted citizen. That is all wrong. Let him come here and enjoy all the privileges that we enjoy, but let him fulfill all the obligations that we are expected to fulfill. After he has adopted it, let this be his country—a country that he will fight for, and die for, if necessary. I am glad to say that the great majority of them do it, but some of them who mingle in politics seem to bank largely on the fact that they are adopted citizens; and that class I am opposed to as much as I am opposed to many other things that I see are popular now.

I know that other speakers will come forward, and when Mr. Beecher and Dr. Newman speak, I hope they will say a few words on the text which I read.

[25] Henry Ward Beecher.
[26] John P. Newman.

**"OLD IRONSIDES"—THE FRIGATE CONSTITUTION—1812**

# OUR NAVY

## HAMPTON L. CARSON

Speech of Hampton L. Carson, delivered at the dinner of the Union League, Philadelphia, April 5, 1899, in honor of Captain Charles E. Clark, U. S. N., late Commander of the battleship "Oregon."

M R. P RESIDENT AND G ENTLEMEN OF THE U NION L EAGUE:—It was my good fortune, some eighteen months ago, to be in the city of Seattle, when the "Monterey" was lying in the harbor under the command of Captain Clark. At the time of my visit clear skies, placid waters and silent guns gave little indication of the awful responsibility that was soon to be imposed upon the gallant commander. My boys, having met him, were, like myself, intensely interested in the outcome of his voyage; and I can say to him that the pulsations of the engines which drove the *Oregon* through fourteen thousand miles of tropic seas were accompanied by the sympathetic beatings of hearts which had learned to love and respect this great captain as he richly deserved.

The American Navy! The most concise tribute that I ever heard paid to the sailors of the United States was contained in the answer of a man from Indiana, who was an applicant for office under General Grant, just after the Civil Service rules had gone into operation. The applicant was apprehensive as to his ability to respond to the questions, but one of his answers captured the board of examiners as well as the president, and he secured the place. The question was, "How many sailors did Great Britain send here, during the war of the Revolution, for the purpose of subduing us?" and the answer was, "More by a——sight than ever got back."

When Louis XIV, in order to check what he perceived to be the growing supremacy of England upon the seas, determined to establish a navy, he sent for his minister Colbert, and said to him, "I wish a navy—how can I create it!" Colbert replied, "Make as many galley slaves as you can." Thereupon every Huguenot who refused to doff his bonnet on the street as the king passed by, every boy of seventeen who could give no account of himself, every vagrant without an occupation, was seized, convicted, and sent to the galleys. Could a navy of heroes be made of galley slaves! The history of the Anglo-Saxon race says "No."

On the twenty-second day of December, 1775, the navy of the United States was born on the waters of our Delaware. On that day Esek Hopkins, of Rhode Island, was placed in command of a little fleet of eight vessels—two of them ships, two of them brigs, the others very much smaller. The English officers sneered in derision at "the fleet of whaleboats." The rattlesnake flag—a yellow flag with a pine tree in the centre and a rattlesnake coiled beneath its branches, with the words "Don't tread on me"—was run to the masthead of the *Providence*, being hauled there by the hands of the first lieutenant, John Paul Jones. That little fleet of eight vessels, mounting only 114 guns, was sent forth to confront a naval power of 112 battleships with 3,714 guns—not a single gun of ours throwing a ball heavier than nine pounds, while five hundred of the English guns threw a weight of metal of double that amount. Wasn't it an audacious thing? Why, it seems to me one of the marvels of human history when I reflect upon what was attempted by the Americans of 1776.

Look at the situation. Thirteen different colonies strung along a narrow strip of coast; three thousand miles of rolling ocean on the one side and three thousand miles of impenetrable wilderness on the other; colonies with infinite diversity of interests—diverse in blood, diverse in conditions of society, diverse in ambition, diverse in pursuits—the English Puritan on the rock of Plymouth, the Knickerbocker Dutch on the shores of the Hudson, the Jersey Quaker on the other side of the Delaware, the Swede extending from here to Wilmington, Maryland bisected by our great bay of the Chesapeake, Virginia cut in half by the same water way, North Carolina and South Carolina lying south of impenetrable swamps as inaccessible to communication as a range of mountains, and farther south the sparsely-settled colony of Georgia. Huguenot, Cavalier, Catholic, Quaker, Dutchman, Puritan, Mennonite, Moravian, and Church of England men; and yet, under the hammer stroke of British oppression, thirteen colonies were welded into one thunderbolt, which was launched at the throne of George III.

That little navy under Hopkins—where were those sailors bred? Read Burke's speech on the conciliation of America. They sprang from the loins of hardy fishermen amidst tumbling fields of ice on the banks of Newfoundland, from those who had speared whales in the tepid waters of Brazil, or who had pursued their gigantic game into the Arctic zone or beneath the light of the Southern Cross. That fleet of eight ships sailed from the Delaware on the twenty-second of December, 1775, and proceeded to the island of New Providence, among the Bahamas. Our colonies and our armies were without arms, without powder, without munitions of war. The very first exploit of the fleet was the capture, on the nineteenth of March, 1776, of 150 cannon, 130 barrels of powder and eight warships, which were carried in triumph into Long Island Sound. But what of American heroism when the soldiers of Howe, of Clinton, of Carleton, and of Gage came here to fight the farmers of Pennsylvania, of Connecticut and Virginia, and the gay cavaliers who loved adventure? The British soldiers had conquered India under Sir Robert Clive and Sir Eyre Coote; they had been the heroes of Plassey and Pondicherry; men who had subjected to British dominion a country almost as extensive as our own fair republic and containing one hundred and ninety millions of souls. Here they found themselves faced by men of their own blood, men in whose breasts burned the spirit and the love of that liberty which was to encircle the heavens. On the glory-crowned heights of Bunker Hill the patriots gazed at the rafters of their own burning dwellings in the town of Charlestown, and heard the cannon shots hurled from British ships against the base of the hill. Three times did scarlet regiments ascend that hill only to be driven back; the voice of that idiot boy, Job Pray, ringing out above the din of battle, "Let them come on to Breed's—the people will teach them the law."

When the evacuation by the British of the metropolis of New England was effected by the troops under the command of a Virginia soldier, General Washington, then for the first time did sectionalism and partisanship and divisions on narrow lines vanish; the patriots who had fought at Bunker Hill were now no longer to be known as the troops of Massachusetts, of Connecticut, or of Rhode Island, but henceforth it was the Continental Army. On the very day when the British were driven out of Boston, John Paul Jones, with that historic rattlesnake flag, and, floating above it, not the Stars and Stripes, but the Stripes with the Union Jack, entered the waters of Great Britain; and then it was seen that an American captain with an American ship and American sailors had the pluck to push out into foreign seas and to beard the British lion in his den. The same channel which had witnessed the victories of De Ruyter and Von Tromp, which was the scene of Blake's victory over the Dutch, and where the father of our great William Penn won his laurels as an admiral, was now the scene of the exploits of an American captain fighting beneath an American flag for American rights inherited from old mother England, who, in a moment of forgetfulness, had sought to deprive her offspring of liberty. I know of no more thrilling incident in revolutionary naval annals than the fight between the *Serapis* and the *Bon Homme Richard*, when Paul Jones, on the burning deck of a sinking ship, lashed his yard arms to those of the enemy and fought hand to hand, man to man, until the British colors struck, and then, under the very cliffs of Old England, were run up for the first time the Stars and Stripes—with a field of blue into which the skillful fingers of Betsy Ross, of Philadelphia, had woven inextinguishable stars; the red stripes typifying the glory, the valor, and the self-sacrifice of the men who died that liberty might live; and the white, emblematic of purity, fitly representing those principles to preserve which these men had sanctified themselves by an immortal self-dedication. And there, too, in the Continental Navy was Richard Dale, the young "Middy," who fought beside Paul Jones; and Joshua Barney; and John Barry; and Nicholas Biddle of Philadelphia, who later, in the gallant little *Randolph*, in order to help a convoyed fleet of American merchantmen to escape, boldly attacked the battleship *Yarmouth*; and when it was found that he was doomed to defeat, blew up his vessel, perishing with all his crew, rather than strike the colors of the newly-born republic.

All honor to the navy of the United States! I never can read of its exploits—peaceful citizen as I am—without my blood bubbling with a joyous sense of exultation at the thought that the flag which has swept the seas, carrying liberty behind it, is the flag which is destined to sweep the seas again and carry liberty, civilization, and all the blessings of free government into benighted islands far, far from hence.

Why, gentlemen, the story of the exploits of our little fleets reads like a romance. At the end of the Revolutionary War eight hundred British ships, fifteen of them battleships, had surrendered to the prowess of the American navy, together with twelve thousand five hundred prisoners captured by less than three thousand men; and in that war our country had produced the boldest admirals that, up to that time, civilization had known, and the greatest fighting naval heroes that the world had seen.

Then came the War of 1812, to establish sailors' rights upon the high seas, when the American navy again proved victor despite overwhelming odds. I have in my possession a list of the British and American vessels at the outbreak of that war; and if I were to represent them by something tangible in order to indicate the proportions of each, I would say, taking this box lid for example (illustrating with the stem of a rose upon the cover of a discarded flower box), that if you were to draw a line across here, near the top, you would have sufficient space in the narrow strip above the dividing line to write the names of all the American ships, while the entire remaining space would not be more than sufficient for the English fleet, which was more than thirty times the size of its antagonist. The ships which under Nelson had fought at the Nile and had won imperishable glory at Trafalgar, coming into our waters, struck their flags time and again. The glorious old "Ironsides" (the *Constitution*) captured the *Guerriere*, the *Java*, the *Cyane*, and *Levant*. The *United States* took the *Macedonian*; the *Wasp* destroyed the *Frolic*, while on the lakes we point with pride to the victories of Perry and MacDonough. When battle after battle had been fought it was found that, of eighteen fixed engagements, seventeen were victories for the Stars and Stripes. And this over the greatest maritime war power of the world!

Philadelphia is honorably associated with the glories of our navy. Our early battleships, though not all built here, were planned and constructed by Joshua Humphreys, a Philadelphian, the predecessor of our great shipbuilder of to-day, Charles H. Cramp.

Need I speak of the navy from 1861 to 1865, or tell of the exploits of those gallant fleets which clove a pathway down the valley of the Ohio, of the Tennessee, and of the Mississippi, in order that liberty might ride unvexed from the lakes to the gulf? Need I dwell upon the part taken by the guest of this evening, who was an officer who fought under Farragut?

In our recent war with Spain there were some who, in doubting moments, yielded to that atrabilious disposition which has been so well described by Mr. Tomkins; who thought that our ships were not strong enough to hazard an encounter with the fleets of Spain. But meanwhile there was doubling "around the Horn" a battleship, with a captain and a crew whose marvelous voyage was attracting the eyes of the world. Night after night we took up the map, traced his course from port to port, and our hearts beat high, our lips were firmly compressed, the color faded from our cheeks with excitement, but our eyes blazed with exultant anticipation as nearer and nearer to Pernambuco did he come. We all now feel, judging of the possibilities by actual achievement, that had Captain Clark encountered the enemy's ships, he could and would have successfully fought and defeated the entire Spanish fleet. He carried his ship ready for instant actions, every man at his post. God bless that crew! God bless those stokers, far down below those decks, confident that the captain who commanded them was on the bridge, and that he would never flinch nor fail in the hour of trial! I have often tried to draw a mental picture of what the scene must have been when the *Oregon* steamed in to join the fleet before Santiago; when the white jackets on the yard-arms tossed their caps in the air, and southern tars gave back to Yankee cheers a lusty welcome to the man who for so long, against all odds, with no encouraging advices, with unknown terrors all about him, had never flinched from duty, and who, when the last summons came, responded in the words of Colonel Newcomb, *Adsum*—"I am here."

On the morning of the third of July, 1898, there stood the frowning Morro Castle, the prison of the glorious Hobson; on the other side the fortress of Estrella; the narrow channel blocked by the wreck of the *Merrimac*; the *Brooklyn*, the *Oregon*, the *Texas*, the *Indiana*, the *Iowa* and the *Massachusetts* all watching that orifice. Then black smoke rolled from the tunnels of the enemy's ships, indicating that the tiger had roused him from his lair and was making a rush for the open sea. Up went the signal on the flagstaff of the *Brooklyn*, "Forward—the enemy is approaching." Then engines moved; then guns thundered their volleys; then sky and sea became black with the smoke of battle; and swiftly steamed the *Oregon* in pursuit of the *Cristobal Colon*. Beneath well-directed shots the monster reeled, like a wounded athlete, to the beach; and then from the flagstaff of the *New York* were displayed those signals now on these walls before your eyes—"1-7-3; cornet; 2m-9m-7m"—which, translated, meant—and we of the League to-night repeat the words—"Well done, *Oregon*."

Captain Clark, the city of Philadelphia has always contributed her share to the building of the navy and to a fitting recognition of the heroes who have commanded our battleships. In the old churchyard of St. Mary's, on Fourth Street, sleep the bones of John Barry; and in the older churchyard of St. Peter's stands the monument to Decatur. We have with us also the ashes of Stewart, who commanded "Old Ironsides" when she captured the *Cyane* and the *Levant*; and we have those of Bainbridge, who captured the *Java*.

In reading of the exploits of the master spirits of the past, I have sometimes wondered whether we had men of to-day who were their equals. My answer is this: I say to soldiers and sailors, whether of our Civil War or of the late war with Spain, you are worthy of your sires, you have caught the inspiration of their glowing deeds, you have taken up the burden which they threw upon your shoulders, and though in time to come you may sleep in unmarked graves, the memory of your deeds will live; and, like your sires, you have become immortal.

To fight for liberty is indeed a privilege. "Disguise thyself as thou wilt, still, Slavery, thou art a bitter draught; and, though thousands in all ages have been made to drink thee, thou art no less bitter on that account. 'Tis thou, O Liberty! thrice sweet and gracious goddess, whose taste is grateful, and ever will be so till nature herself shall change. No tint of words can spot thy snowy mantle, nor chemic power turn thy scepter into iron. With thee to smile upon him, as he eats his crust, the swain is happier than the monarch from whose courts thou art exiled." So wrote Laurence Sterne.

And then Rufus Choate: "To form and uphold a state, it is not enough that our judgments should believe it to be useful; the better part of our affections should feel it to be lovely. It is not enough that our arithmetic should compute its value and find it high; our hearts should hold it priceless—above all things rich and rare—dearer than health and beauty, brighter than all the order of the stars." In contemplating those mysterious dispensations of Providence by which the light which broke upon this continent two hundred years ago is now penetrating and illuminating the darkest corners of the earth, it will be a supreme satisfaction for us to know that our children and our children's children will have set for their imitation and encouragement the example of the heroism, the manliness, the courage, the patriotism and the modesty of the captains of to-day.

**LATEST TYPE OF DREADNAUGHT**

# THE PATRIOTISM OF PEACE

## WILLIAM J. BRYAN

Address by William Jennings Bryan delivered in London, in the
Royal Gallery of the House of Lords, on July 26, 1906, at the session of the Interparliamentary Union or Peace Congress. It is giv-
en here by special permission of Mr. Bryan and his publishers —
Funk and Wagnalls Company, New York and London.

I regret that I cannot speak to you in the language which is usually employed
in this body, but I know only one language, the language of my own country, and
you will pardon me if I use that. I desire in the first place to express my appreciation of the courtesy shown me by Lord Weardale, our president, and by Baron
von Plener, the chairman of the committee which framed the model treaty. The
latter has framed this substitute embodying both of the ideas (investigation and
meditation) which were presented yesterday. I recognize the superior wisdom
and the greater experience of this learned committee which has united the two
propositions, and I thank this body also for the opportunity to say just a word in
defense of my part of the resolution. I cannot say that it is a new idea, for since it
was presented yesterday I have learned that the same idea in substance was presented last year at Brussels by Mr. Bartholdt, of my own country, who has been so
conspicuous in his efforts to promote peace, and I am very glad that I can follow
in his footsteps in the urging of this amendment. I may add also that it is in line
with the suggestion made by the honorable prime minister of Great Britain, Sir
Henry Campbell-Bannerman, in that memorable and epoch-making speech of yesterday, in that speech which contained several sentences any one of which would
have justified the assembling of this Interparliamentary Union — any one of which
would have compensated us all for coming here. In that splendid speech he expressed the hope that the scope of arbitration treaties might be enlarged. He said:

> "Gentlemen, I fervently trust that before long the principles
> of arbitration may win such confidence as to justify its extension
> to a wider field of international differences. We have already seen
> how questions arousing passion and excitement have attained a
> solution, not necessarily by means of arbitration in the strict sense
> of the word, by referring them to such a tribunal as that which
> reported on the North Sea incident; and I would ask you whether,
> it may not be worth while carefully to consider, before the next
> Congress meets at The Hague, the various forms in which dif-
> ferences might be submitted, with a view to opening the door as

wide as possible to every means which might in any degree contribute to moderate or compose such differences."

This amendment is in harmony with this suggestion. The resolution is in the form of a postscript to the treaty, but like the postscripts to some letters it contains a very vital subject—in fact, I am not sure but the postscript in this case is as important as the letter itself, for it deals with those questions which have defied arbitration. Certain questions affecting the honor or integrity of a nation are generally thought to be outside of the jurisdiction of a court of arbitration, and these are the questions which have given trouble. Passion is not often aroused by questions that do not affect a nation's integrity or honor, but for fear these questions may arise arbitration is not always employed where it might be. The first advantage, then, of this resolution is that it secures an investigation of the facts, and if you can but separate these facts from the question of honor, the chances are 100-to-1 that you can settle both the fact and the question of honor without war. There is, therefore, a great advantage in an investigation that brings out the facts, for disputed facts between nations, as between friends, are the cause of most disagreements.

The second advantage of this investigation is that it gives time for calm consideration. That has already been well presented by the gentlemen who has preceded me, Baron von Plener. I need not say to you that man excited is a very different animal from man calm, and that questions ought to be settled, not by passion, but by deliberation. If this resolution would do nothing else but give time for reflection and deliberation, there would be sufficient reason for its adoption. If we can but stay the hand of war until conscience can assert itself, war will be made more remote. When men are mad they swagger around and tell what they can do; when they are calm they consider what they ought to do.

The third advantage of this investigation is that it gives opportunity to mobilize public opinion of the compelling of a peaceful settlement and that is an advantage not to be overlooked. Public opinion is coming to be more and more a power in the world. One of the greatest statesmen of my country—Thomas Jefferson, and if it would not offend I would say I believe him to be the greatest statesman the world has produced—said that if he had to choose between a government without newspapers and newspapers without a government, he would rather risk the newspapers without a government. You may call it an extravagant statement, and yet it presents an idea, and that idea is that public opinion is a controlling force. I am glad that the time is coming when public opinion is to be more and more powerful; glad that the time is coming when the moral sentiment of one nation will influence the action of other nations; glad that the time is coming when the world will realize that a war between the two nations affects others than the nations involved; glad that the time is coming when the world will insist that nations settle their differences by some peaceful means. If time is given for the marshaling of the force of public opinion peace will be promoted. This resolution is presented, therefore, for the reasons that it gives an opportunity to investigate the facts, and to separate them from the question of honor, that it gives time for the calming of passion, and that it gives time for the formation of a controlling public sentiment.

I will not disguise the fact that I consider this resolution a long step in the direction of peace, nor will I disguise the fact that I am here because I want this Interparliamentary Union to take just as long a step as possible in the direction of universal peace. We meet in a famous hall, and looking down upon us from these walls are pictures that illustrate not only the glory that is to be won in war, but the horrors that follow war. There is a picture of one of the great figures in English history (pointing to the fresco by Maclise of the death of Nelson). Lord Nelson is represented as dying, and around him are the mangled forms of others. I understand that war brings out certain virtues. I am aware that it gives opportunity for the display of great patriotism; I am aware that the example of men who give their lives for their country is inspiring; but I venture to say there is as much inspiration in a noble life as there is in a heroic death, and I trust that one of the results of this Interparliamentary Union will be to emphasize the doctrine that a life devoted to the public, and ever flowing, like a spring, with good, exerts an influence upon the human race and upon the destiny of the world as great as any death in war. And if you will permit me to mention one whose career I watched with interest and whose name I revere, I will say that, in my humble judgment, the sixty-four years of spotless public service of William Ewart Gladstone will, in years to come, be regarded as rich an ornament to the history of this nation as the life of any man who poured out his blood upon a battlefield.

All movements in the interest of peace have back of them the idea of brotherhood. If peace is to come in this world, it will come because people more and more clearly recognize the indissoluble tie that binds each human being to every other. If we are to build permanent peace it must be on the foundation of the brotherhood of men. A poet has described how in the Civil War that divided our country into two hostile camps a generation ago—in one battle a soldier in one line thrust his bayonet through a soldier in the opposing line, and how, when he stooped to draw it out, he recognized in the face of the fallen one the face of his own brother. And then the poet describes the feeling of horror that overwhelmed the survivor when he realized that he had taken the life of one who was the child of the same parents and the companion of his boyhood. It was a pathetic story, but is it too much to hope that as years go by we will begin to understand that the whole human race is but a larger family?

It is not too much to hope that as years go by human sympathy will expand until this feeling of unity will not be confined to the members of a family or to the members of a clan or of a community or state, but shall be world-wide. It is not too much to hope that we, in this assembly, possibly by this resolution, may hasten the day when we shall feel so appalled at the thought of the taking of any human life that we shall strive to raise all questions to a level where the settlement will be by reason and not by force.

# A PLEA FOR UNIVERSAL PEACE
## GEORGE W. NORRIS

The following extracts are from an address delivered by George W. Norris, United States senator from Nebraska, at Chautauquas and on lecture courses throughout the country for several years. It is one of the most logical and practical plans for universal peace ever proposed. It was prepared when the civilized world was at peace immediately following the peace treaty between Russia and Japan. David Starr Jordan declares that "military efficiency" is the principal cause of the present European war. A serious and honest study of how to preserve peace and how to avoid war cannot help but bring good results. This is the purpose of Senator Norris's lecture. For a further study of this most important subject, the reader is referred to Sumner's great oration on "The True Grandeur of Nations," to various speeches and monographs by Andrew Carnegie, and to numerous other publications, recently issued, regarding the patriotism of peace.

The greatest disgrace of the present century is that war between civilized nations is still a possibility. That such a barbarous condition should exist in the civilized world is painful to every lover of humanity and to every believer in the great brotherhood of man.

Every civilized country of the world requires its subjects to submit their differences and disputes to tribunals and courts that have been organized under the forms of law for their settlement and yet these same nations violate the principle of law which they compel their subjects to obey. The citizen must maintain his rights and settle his grievances before tribunals organized according to law, upon principles of justice and of right. Kings and rulers settle their disputes upon the field of battle without regard to right, without regard to justice, and upon the erroneous and barbarous theory that might makes right. It is to be regretted that the great advance that has been made from barbarism by the different nations of the world by which the disputes and controversies arising within each nation are settled according to forms of law upon the principles of justice and equality, has not extended to the settlement of disputes between the nations themselves. Why is it that rulers, who are able to settle all controversies within the countries they control are not able to settle controversies between those countries?

Humanity is broader than nationality and embraces within its scope the entire world. The measure of human happiness will not be full, the heights of national glory will not be reached until we can look over the world and in the words of the scripture, truthfully say of every citizen of every civilized nation—"Is he not after all, my brother?"

Why then should there be war? I know that it can truthfully be claimed that this cruel and heartless demon has settled many questions of world-wide importance, but it never settled one on any principle of equity, morality, or justice. In modern times its decree has been more often right than wrong, because the great spirit of public sentiment when once aroused has not only furnished money and men for the right, but it has thoroughly imbued the hearts of its soldiers with a determination and a bravery that have done much to place the victory where it properly belonged. But what a sacrifice of human life and treasure. I do not want to be understood as claiming that all the wars of history were wrong or could have been avoided. Some of them were carried on for liberty, some were waged for mercy and some were fought for humanity. The soldier, not only of our own land, but of other countries as well, is entitled to all the consideration and all the honor and glory that humanity can give or bestow. I am however proclaiming against the conditions existing in modern civilized times that make war not only sometimes necessary, but at any time possible.

But the question recurs again—what is a practical way to solve the difficulty? Who shall take the first step? Who can take the first step with the assurance that beneficial results will follow? What nation to-day occupies such a unique position in civilization that it can step out into the open and say to all the civilized world—"We are willing to submit to peaceful arbitration every international dispute, every international controversy not only of the present but of the future as well." What nation in assuming this position can command not only the respect and belief of other nations in the integrity and the honesty of its purpose, but can also receive the respect and approval of humanity's peace loving sentiment, that will go far towards impelling the balance of the civilized world to accept the proffered hand of universal brotherhood!

If we study the history of European nations, we will find a trace at least of jealousy between them that has come down from the days of barbarism. In ancient times the king, who was then supposed to possess, and is still suspicioned to have, some attributes of Divinity, ruled only over such territory as he was able to hold in subjection. He broke no law of nations if, without notice, cause or provocation, he made war upon his neighbor in an attempt to conquer and subdue additional territory. He violated no principle of government if in carrying out his purpose he resorted to trickery, chicanery, and dishonesty. The result was that every ruler was suspicious of every other ruler.

This suspiciousness and lack of confidence anciently existing between kings, and permeating the framework of every European nation, has, in a lessening and decreasing degree, come down to the present day. It exists now—unconsciously perhaps—but exists nevertheless, and must be taken into consideration whenever any European nation makes a proposition to other European nations for the settlement of any great international question. This condition was well paraphrased by a great European statesman in comparing European conditions with those of America, when he referred to it as American boldness and European suspiciousness.

In the new world where our government's leadership and controlling influence are recognized and acknowledged by all the world, these conditions do not obtain. Here the divine right of kings has never been recognized. We have not only disclaimed the right of conquest ourselves, but we have refused to recognize it in others. We have not only refused to recognize this right in the strong nation, but we have protected the weak nation against it. Moreover we have shown to the world our unselfish devotion to that principle to the extent of sacrificing life and treasure in the defense of the weak against the strong—the protection of the down-trodden and oppressed against oppression. Our entire national life has been emblematic of an unselfish respect for the rights of other nations, and is not tainted with that suspiciousness which has come down to others from ancient times. Our position among the nations of the world was well illustrated by what happened in the war between Russia and Japan.

When these two great nations had gotten each other by the throat and were struggling in mortal combat, the entire world was aroused to admiration by the action of America's great president. Neither one of the warring nations had expressed any desire for peace. Neither one had shown any disposition to cease the conflict. Neither one had asked for any intercession, and yet in the midst of the bloody conflict, when America's voice was heard, they both halted, they both ceased, and they both obeyed.

It was because they knew—all the world knew—that in the voice which called them from the battlefield to reason's court there was no taint of selfishness; that in that call there was no suspicion of an ulterior or dishonorable motive, but that in the heart of the great statesman, whose voice they heeded, there was only the purity of a humane effort to bring about the welfare of all. From the very nature of the development of other nations from the barbarism of ancient times it is quite apparent that no other ruler of the civilized world could have made that proposition with the same successful results. In response to the friendly intervention of the American Government, Russia and Japan appointed commissioners to agree upon terms of peace.

While these commissioners were in session on American soil, a notable assemblage for the advancement of international arbitration was in session at Brussels, the capital of Belgium. At this meeting of the Interparliamentary Union there were representatives from practically every civilized country in the world except Russia and Japan. We watched with hopeful anxiety the reports which the cable brought us of the progress that was being made by these peace commissioners at Portsmouth. In that assemblage, composed of representatives from two continents, there was a unanimous wish, a united hope, a fervent prayer that America's intervention would prove successful.

As a fitting close of that great international conference the representatives of Belgium invited all the delegates to a reception held in that historic building where the cohorts of Napoleon were assembled in revelry on the eve of Waterloo. The rooms were decorated with the colors of all nations. The finest band of Belgium was playing her national air. In the midst of it the music suddenly ceased. All eyes were turned to the rostrum. We saw the leader of the band seize from the decorations of the hall the American flag, and using it as a baton, he waved it over the heads of the musicians, and in answer to his action there burst forth the rapturous strains of "The Star Spangled Banner."

For a moment, and a moment only, there was silence, and then there burst forth a roar of applause which clearly indicated that everyone there understood, that beneath the fathomless deep the electric spark had brought the welcome news that on the shores of America an agreement for peace had been signed. On the occasion of nearly one hundred years before the revelry was interrupted by the booming of cannon, but on this occasion it was the joyous message that under the leadership of America the peace of the world had been established. That was an occasion, my countrymen, when it was greater to be an American citizen than to wear a crown.

Heretofore one of the greatest obstacles to the peaceful settlement of international difficulties, and to the submission of such controversies to arbitration, has been that the offense has been committed, or the controversy has arisen before any rule for its settlement has been provided, or any tribunal for its determination has been selected. This ex post facto machinery for the settlement of differences is not only unreasonable and illogical, but it has been guarded against by all the civilized nations of the earth in the regulation and management of their own internal affairs. When disagreeing nations are aroused to anger by the excitement and the prejudice of the people on account of real or imaginary wrong, it is a poor time indeed to attempt to agree upon a fair method of settlement, or to exercise that calm deliberation which should be invoked in the selection of the arbitrators.

The treaty of arbitration should be general and apply to all disputes. It should be negotiated in time of profound peace, and not with reference to any particular controversy. Its judges should be selected in time of peace and their terms of office should be permanent. In order that they might be removed from, and uninfluenced by, any bias or prejudice they should be appointed for life, and while holding this great international commission they should be prohibited from accepting or holding any other office or emolument from any government.

The treaty, however, should specifically provide that these international judges could be appointed and selected as members of any other international arbitration tribunal, and in accordance with this provision each government would undoubtedly select the same men as judges for each arbitration treaty into which it entered.

To illustrate—if our government entered into such a treaty with the German Empire, and afterwards into a similar treaty with France, we would select the same arbitrators under the treaty with France that we had named in carrying out the provisions of the treaty with Germany, and in any subsequent arbitration treaty with any other nation, the same men would again be named as our arbitrators.

There is little doubt but what all other nations would pursue a similar course.

This would give us an international court that would command the absolute respect of all mankind and the confidence of all civilization. Its judges would be free from any bias, prejudice or excitement that might exist in either one or both of the contending nations. Instead of representing one government as against the other they would in fact, without partiality and with equal justice, represent both of the contending parties. Their life work would be the study of international questions. They would become learned—yea, experts—in international law and the administration of international justice. If each nation selected the same judges in each of its arbitration treaties, the world would have a list—a school—of international jurists devoting their time, their energies and their lives to the study of international questions and the settlement of international disputes. In the hands of these men the peace of the civilized world would be safe and secure.

The treaty of arbitration would undoubtedly provide for an equal number of arbitrators from each of the contracting parties. It likewise would, and undoubtedly should, provide for the selection of additional members of the court in cases where the judges were equally divided on any question submitted to them. A wise provision would be to let the permanent judges themselves select the additional arbitrators, and with this list of great international jurists from which to make a choice, how small the possibility of error, and how great would be the probability of a wise selection. As a matter of fact it would seldom be necessary for this provision of the treaty to be acted on. Not once in a lifetime would the members of such a court be divided along the lines of nationality. The judges of this court, occupying this dignified, exalted and unparalleled position before the world, would be farther removed from bias and prejudice than any court that has ever been instituted in the history of mankind. Its decisions would become precedents for future action. It would not be long until we would have a line of decisions, that would eliminate the uncertainty of international law which has existed in the past. A question once determined by this great court would be accepted by the world as the law for the future, and the result would be that we would not only have an international tribunal for the peaceful settlement and determination of all international questions, but their decisions would become the beacon lights of peace for future generations, whose rays of wisdom and of reason would light up the dark waters of international jurisprudence, mark out the course of safety for every ship of state, and warn her mariners of the shoals of disaster.

There is no ground whatever for the belief which prevails somewhat that the members of such a court would always follow the contention of their own country. Even under the present cumbersome and illogical method of selecting arbitrators we have a recent illustration that men great enough to fill positions of this kind, realizing the dignity and responsibility of the position, will rise above the clamor of their own countrymen and decide the question at issue upon its merits. I refer to the Alaskan boundary dispute between the United States and Great Britain. We have also an illustration of this point in our own country.

Our national government is composed of sovereign states. State pride is an attribute of practically all our citizens. Its influence has compelled men to honestly do all kinds of unreasonable things. For it men have given up their property and sacrificed their lives. Yet this prejudice has never reached our judiciary. Every United States judge is a citizen of some state. They try cases between different states, pass on disputes existing between a sovereign state and the citizens of another state, and settle controversies arising between the citizens of one state and the citizens of another state. Our judges have been criticized on nearly all possible grounds, often no doubt without reason, sometimes perhaps with good cause, but in the entire history of our country, there has never yet been made the charge that any one of these judges has been influenced in his official conduct by pride of his native or adopted state. Man is often unconsciously influenced and controlled by his associations, his habits and the environments of earlier life. Their influence has become a part of the man. But the history of jurisprudence will show that judges have seldom, if ever, been moved or influenced in official action by the excitement, the clamor or the prejudice of the citizenship if it was beyond the power of that citizenship to reward or punish.

It is unnecessary to provide any method for the enforcement of the decrees of an international court. It is safe to trust to the honor of the governments interested, and to the enlightened public sentiment of the civilized world for the honest enforcement in good faith of every such judgment and decree. This has been frequently demonstrated in the past. In all the history of the world there has never been an instance where an offending nation has failed to carry out in good faith the judgment of an international court.

In America the friends of international arbitration are not united as they should be. The division comes about principally on account of a disagreement as to what should be the size of our navy. There are some who believe that we should make but a small annual increase in our navy, and some of these are inclined to criticize those who advocate a large navy and to claim that such conduct is inconsistent with international arbitration. While I have been one of those who usually have favored a small yearly increase in our naval vessels, yet I am frank to admit that under present conditions, there is much sound logic in the argument that the greatest and best assurance of international peace, is to be always prepared for war. It is well too, to remember that an unbiased and unprejudiced tribunal in a foreign land has recently given an international trophy—the world's prize—to the greatest American exponent of a large navy, for having during the year for which the prize was given, accomplished more for international peace, than any other living man. It is not my intention to discuss this subject. It is not necessary to decide it for the purposes of the present discussion. It is of importance when considering the subject of national defense and national finances, but it has no decisive influence upon the question of international arbitration. The man who favors a small navy, and the man who favors a large one can consistently work side by side for the advancement of international peace. The size of the navy that we should maintain is a question upon which the minds of wise and patriotic men may honestly differ. Everybody admits that we should keep and maintain an ample and sufficient navy, and that annual additions thereto are necessary to maintain its efficiency. But, the terms "adequate navy," "sufficient navy" and "large navy" are very indefinite, and convey entirely different ideas to different people. What one man might regard as a small navy, another one equally as wise would regard as entirely too large. What one person would consider a small and inadequate annual addition to our navy, others, equally as patriotic, would regard as unreasonable and extravagant. A man's ideas on this disputed and unsettled question can not consistently be urged against the sincerity of his purpose when he advocates international arbitration.

But while the friends of international arbitration may honestly disagree as to the strength of the army and the size of the navy that should be maintained in times of peace, there is no disagreement in the condemnation of the conditions which make it necessary to maintain a large army and navy. These conditions are relics of barbarism. They are not founded upon any wisdom, reason, or justice. They exist only because the great men of to-day, who hold the destinies of nations in their hands have not met upon the broad plane of equality and agreed upon their abolishment.

Heretofore the cry of international arbitration has come mainly from those who were moved by the idea of philanthropy, of mercy and of humanity. It will not be long until these influences will be joined by all the commercial interests of civilization and all the tax-payers of the world. For the fiscal year (1907) in our own country there was appropriated from the national treasury nearly four hundred millions of dollars on account of war. Over sixty-five per cent. of the revenues of our national government are spent on account of our wars of the past, or in preparation for war in the future. Every time our government raises a dollar by taxation more than sixty-five cents of it is demanded as a tribute by this blood thirsty demon.

Our situation is only a fair illustration of what exists everywhere in the world. In round numbers about one-half of the money raised by taxation in the leading civilized nations of the world is spent, either in the payment of obligations of past wars, or in the preparation for war in the future. The expense of this preparation is increasing at a wonderful rate. Our government expends about the same amount of money as the other leading nations of the world in the preparation for war in the future, but for the expenses of wars that are past it expends more than all the other nations combined. The expenses of our past wars, consisting chiefly and mainly of pensions, are just, and no one would cut them down, excepting as they will be curtailed by the hand of Time as he gathers into his fold our heroes of the past. We will therefore eliminate the past from the financial consideration of the question. During a single year of peace, Great Britain, Germany, France, and the United States spent nearly one billion of dollars in making preparation for war. All the money in the United States would only pay this enormous expense for a little more than two years. The people of these highly civilized countries, while in profound peace, were taxing themselves to death, in order that the survivors might kill each other according to the most modern methods of modern warfare with the most modern weapons of human destruction.

As startling and astounding as these figures are, they do not tell one half of the story. Human life cannot be measured in dollars and cents; broken hearts cannot be healed by the appropriation of money; human suffering and misery cannot be alleviated by financial consideration, and humanity stands helpless in the face of death and destruction. At the fireside of practically every home in Christendom, there is a vacant chair, made so by war. For every vacant chair there was a ruined hearthstone; for every hearthstone there was a sorrowing widow; and for every widow there is a fatherless child. For every penny spent for war there is a sigh of grief; for every shilling there is a tear of sorrow; and for every dollar there is a broken heart. The amount expended on this account in the civilized world, in one year would give shelter to every pauper, a home to every unfortunate, and an education to every child. At the present rate of increasing expense it will not be long until this great chain will break of its own weight; until every nation will become bankrupt and every tax-payer will become a pauper. As this time approaches, the forces of international peace will become more numerous and more powerful. Humanity will shake off the shackles of barbarism and defy the God of War upon his throne. In this battle of reason, that tyrant of oppression, that ruler of ignorance, that demon of superstition, in whose decree there is no mercy, in whose judgment there is no justice, will be driven from his throne, and relegated beyond the portals of a universal peace, to be remembered only as a horrible nightmare of an unholy and an unrighteous past.

THE ADDRESS AT GETTYSBURG

# LINCOLN'S GETTYSBURG ADDRESS

## ABRAHAM LINCOLN

Fourscore and seven years ago our fathers brought forth upon this continent a new nation, conceived in liberty, and dedicated to the proposition that all men are created equal. Now we are engaged in a great civil war, testing whether that nation, or any nation so conceived and so dedicated, can long endure.

We are met on a great battlefield of that war. We have come to dedicate a portion of that field as the final resting-place for those who here gave their lives that that nation might live. It is altogether fitting and proper that we should do this. But in a larger sense we cannot dedicate, we cannot consecrate, we cannot hallow this ground. The brave men, living and dead, who struggled here have consecrated it far above our power to add or detract. The world will little note, nor long remember, what we say here; but it can never forget what they did here.

It is for us, the living, rather to be dedicated here to the unfinished work which they who fought here have thus far so nobly advanced. It is rather for us to be here dedicated to the great task remaining before us, that from these honored dead we take increased devotion to that cause for which they here gave the last full measure of devotion; that we here highly resolve that these dead shall not have died in vain; that this nation, under God, shall have a new birth of freedom, and that government of the people, by the people, and for the people, shall not perish from the earth.

# PRESIDENT WILSON'S NEUTRALITY PROC-LAMATION

## WOODROW WILSON

This proclamation is in strict keeping with Washington's counsel. It is one of the greatest of President Wilson's state papers and probably did more than any one act of his administration in keeping the United States from becoming involved in the European war.

My Fellow Countrymen:—I suppose that every thoughtful man in America has asked himself, during these last troubled weeks, what influence the European war may exert upon the United States, and I take the liberty of addressing a few words to you in order to point out that it is entirely within our own choice what its effects upon us will be and to urge very earnestly upon you the sort of speech and conduct which will best safeguard the Nation against distress and disaster.

The effect of the war upon the United States will depend upon what American citizens say and do. Every man who really loves America will act and speak in the true spirit of neutrality, which is the spirit of impartiality and fairness and friendliness to all concerned. The spirit of the Nation in this critical matter will be determined largely by what individuals and society and those gathered in public meetings do and say, upon what newspapers and magazines contain, upon what ministers utter in their pulpits, and men proclaim as their opinions on the street.

The people of the United States are drawn from many nations, and chiefly from the nations now at war. It is natural and inevitable that there should be the utmost variety of sympathy and desire among them with regard to the issues and circumstances of the conflict. Some will wish one nation, others another, to succeed in the momentous struggle. It will be easy to excite passion and difficult to allay it. Those responsible for exciting it will assume a heavy responsibility, responsibility for no less a thing than that the people of the United States, whose love of their country and whose loyalty to its government should unite them as Americans all, bound in honor and affection to think first of her and her interests, may be divided in camps of hostile opinion, hot against each other, involved in the war itself in impulse and opinion if not in action.

Such divisions among us would be fatal to our peace of mind and might seriously stand in the way of the proper performance of our duty as the one great nation at peace, the one people holding itself ready to play a part of impartial mediation and speak the counsels of peace and accommodation, not as a partisan, but as a friend.

I venture, therefore, my fellow countrymen, to speak a solemn word of warning to you against that deepest, most subtle, most essential breach of neutrality which may spring out of partisanship, out of passionately taking sides. The United States must be neutral in fact as well as in name during these days that are to try men's souls. We must be impartial in thought as well as in action, must put a curb upon our sentiments as well as upon every transaction that might be construed as a preference of one party to the struggle before another.

My thought is of America. I am speaking, I feel sure, the earnest wish and purpose of every thoughtful American that this great country of ours, which is, of course, the first in our thoughts and in our hearts, should show herself in this time of peculiar trial a Nation fit beyond others to exhibit the fine poise of undisturbed judgment, the dignity of self-control, the efficiency of dispassionate action; a Nation that neither sits in judgment upon others nor is disturbed in her own counsels and which keeps herself fit and free to do what is honest and disinterested and truly serviceable for the peace of the world.

Shall we not resolve to put upon ourselves the restraints which will bring to our people the happiness and the great and lasting influence for peace we covet for them?

August 18, 1914.

# POETRY OF PATRIOTISM

**THE STATUE OF LIBERTY**
New York Harbor

# **CONCORD HYMN** [27]

## **RALPH WALDO EMERSON**

By the rude bridge that arched the flood,
Their flag to April's breeze unfurled,
Here once the embattled farmers stood,
And fired the shot heard round the world.

The foe long since in silence slept;
Alike the conqueror silent sleeps;
And Time the ruined bridge has swept
Down the dark stream which seaward creeps.

On this green bank, by this soft stream,
We set to-day a votive stone;
That memory may their dead redeem,
When, like our sires, our sons are gone.

Spirit, that made those heroes dare
To die, and leave their children free,
Bid Time and Nature gently spare
The shaft we raise to them and thee.

Ralph Waldo Emerson

[27] By Ralph Waldo Emerson, at the dedication, April 19, 1836, of the monument erected at Concord in honor of the patriots who fell in the battle of Lexington sixty-one years before.

# WARREN'S ADDRESS

## JOHN PIERPONT

Stand! the ground's your own, my braves!
Will ye give it up to slaves?
Will ye look for greener graves?
Hope ye mercy still?
What's the mercy despots feel?
Hear it in that battle peal!
Read it on yon bristling steel!
Ask it—ye who will.

Fear ye foes who kill for hire?
Will ye to your homes retire?
Look behind you!—they're afire!
And, before you, see
Who have done it! From the vale
On they come!—and will ye quail?
Leaden rain and iron hail
Let their welcome be!

In the God of battles trust!
Die we may—and die we must;
But, oh, where can dust to dust
Be consigned so well,
As where heaven its dews shall shed
On the martyred patriot's bed,
And the rocks shall raise their head,
Of his deeds to tell?

John Pierpont

# PATRIOTISM

## SIR WALTER SCOTT

Breathes there the man, with soul so dead,
Who never to himself hath said,
This is my own, my native land!
Whose heart hath ne'er within him burned,
As home his footsteps he hath turned
From wandering on a foreign strand!
If such there breathe, go, mark him well;
For him no minstrel raptures swell;
High though his titles, proud his name,
Boundless his wealth as wish can claim;
Despite those titles, power, and pelf,
The wretch, concentered all in self,
Living, shall forfeit fair renown,
And, doubly dying, shall go down
To the vile dust, from whence he sprung,
Unwept, unhonored, and unsung.

Sir Walter Scott

# THE STAR-SPANGLED BANNER
## FRANCIS SCOTT KEY

Oh, say, can you see, by the dawn's early light,
What so proudly we hailed at the twilight's last gleaming,
Whose broad stripes and bright stars, through the perilous fight,
O'er the ramparts we watched were so gallantly streaming?
And the rocket's red glare, the bombs bursting in air,
Gave proof through the night that our flag was still there:
Oh, say, does that Star-Spangled Banner yet wave
O'er the land of the free and the home of the brave?

On that shore dimly seen through the mists of the deep,
Where the foe's haughty host in dread silence reposes,
What is that which the breeze, o'er the towering steep,
As it fitfully blows, now conceals, now discloses!
Now it catches the gleam of the morning's first beam,
In full glory reflected now shines on the stream:
'Tis the Star-Spangled Banner, Oh, long may it wave
O'er the land of the free and the home of the brave.

And where is that band who so vauntingly swore
That the havoc of war and the battle's confusion
A home and a country should leave us no more!
Their blood has washed out their foul footsteps' pollution;
No refuge should save the hireling and slave
From the terror of flight or the gloom of the grave:
And the Star-Spangled Banner in triumph doth wave
O'er the land of the free and the home of the brave.

Oh, thus be it ever when freemen shall stand
Between their loved homes and war's desolation.
Blest with victory and peace, may the Heaven-rescued land
Praise the power that hath made and preserved us a nation.
Then conquer we must, when our cause it is just,
And this be our motto, "In God is our trust":
And the Star-Spangled Banner in triumph shall wave
O'er the land of the free and the home of the brave.

Francis Scott Key

# MY COUNTRY

## SAMUEL F. SMITH

My country, 'tis of thee,
Sweet land of liberty,
Of thee I sing.
Land where my fathers died,
Land of the pilgrims' pride,
From every mountain side
Let freedom ring!

My native country! Thee—
Land of the noble free,—
Thy name I love;
I love thy rocks and rills,
Thy woods and templed hills;
My heart with rapture thrills
Like that above.

Let music swell the breeze,
And ring from all the trees
Sweet freedom's song.
Let mortal tongues awake;
Let all that breathe partake;
Let rocks their silence break,—
The sound prolong.

Our fathers' God, to Thee,
Author of liberty,
To Thee we sing;
Long may our land be bright
With freedom's holy light;
Protect us by Thy might,
Great God, our King!

Samuel F. Smith

# THE AMERICAN FLAG

## JOSEPH RODMAN DRAKE

When Freedom, from her mountain height,
Unfurled her standard to the air,
She tore the azure robe of night,
And set the stars of glory there.
She mingled with its gorgeous dyes
The milky baldric of the skies,
And striped its pure celestial white
With streakings of the morning light.

Then, from his mansion in the sun,
She called her eagle bearer down,
And gave into his mighty hand
The symbol of her chosen land.
Flag of the free heart's hope and home,
By angel hands to valor given!
Thy stars have lit the welkin dome,
And all thy hues were born in heaven.

Forever float that standard sheet!
Where breathes the foe but falls before us,
With Freedom's soil beneath our feet,
And Freedom's banner streaming o'er us!

Joseph Rodman Drake

# SONG OF MARION'S MEN
## WILLIAM CULLEN BRYANT

Our band is few but true and tried,
Our leader frank and bold;
The British soldier trembles
When Marion's name is told.
Our fortress is the good greenwood,
Our tent the cypress tree;
We know the forest round us,
As seamen know the sea.
We know its walls of thorny vines,
Its glades of reedy grass,
Its safe and silent islands
Within the dark morass.

Woe to the English soldiery
That little dread us near!
On them shall light at midnight
A strange and sudden fear
When, waking to their tents on fire,
They grasp their arms in vain,
And they who stand to face us
Are beat to earth again;
And they who fly in terror deem
A mighty host behind,
And hear the tramp of thousands
Upon the hollow wind.

Then sweet the hour that brings release
From danger and from toil:
We talk the battle over,
And share the battle's spoil.
The woodland rings with laugh and shout,
As if a hunt were up,
And woodland flowers are gathered
To crown the soldier's cup.
With merry songs we mock the wind
That in the pine-top grieves,
And slumber long and sweetly

On beds of oaken leaves.

Well knows the fair and friendly moon
The band that Marion leads—
The glitter of their rifles,
The scampering of their steeds.
'Tis life to guide the fiery barb
Across the moonlight plain;
'Tis life to feel the night wind
That lifts his tossing mane.
A moment in the British camp—
A moment—and away,
Back to the pathless forest,
Before the peep of day.

Grave men there are by broad Santee,
Grave men with hoary hairs;
Their hearts are all with Marion,
For Marion are their prayers.
And lovely ladies greet our band,
With kindliest welcoming,
With smiles like those of summer,
And tears like those of spring.
For them we wear these trusty arms,
And lay them down no more
Till we have driven the Briton,
Forever from our shore.

William Cullen Bryant

# THE OLD CONTINENTALS
## GUY HUMPHREYS MCMASTER

In their ragged regimentals
Stood the old Continentals,
Yielding not,
When the grenadiers were lunging,
And like hail fell the plunging
Cannon shot;
When the files
Of the isles,
From the smoky night encampment, bore the banner of the rampant
Unicorn;
And grummer, grummer, grummer, rolled the roll of the drummer
Through the morn!

Then with eyes to the front all,
And with guns horizontal,
Stood our sires;
And the balls whistled deadly,
And in streams flashing redly,
Blazed the fires:
As the roar
On the shore
Swept the strong battle breakers o'er the green-sodded acres
Of the plain;
And louder, louder, louder, cracked the black gunpowder,
Cracking amain!

Now like smiths at their forges
Worked the red St. George's
Cannoneers,
And the villainous saltpetre
Rung a fierce, discordant meter
Round their ears;
As the swift
Storm drift,
With hot sweeping anger, came the horseguards' clangor
On our flanks;
Then higher, higher, higher, burned the old-fashioned fire

Through the ranks!

Then the bareheaded colonel
Galloped through the white infernal
Powder cloud;
And his broadsword was swinging,
And his brazen throat was ringing
Trumpet-loud;
Then the blue
Bullets flew,
And the trooper jackets redden at the touch of the leaden
Rifle breath;
And rounder, rounder, rounder, roared the iron six-pounder,
Hurling death!

Guy Humphreys McMaster

# THE SWORD OF BUNKER HILL
## WM. ROSS WALLACE

He lay upon his dying bed;
His eye was growing dim,
When with a feeble voice he called
His weeping son to him:
"Weep not, my boy!" the vet'ran said,
"I bow to Heaven's high will—
But quickly from yon antlers bring
The sword of Bunker Hill."

The sword was brought, the soldier's eye
Lit with a sudden flame;
And as he grasped the ancient blade,
He murmured Warren's name;
Then said, "My boy, I leave you gold—
But what is richer still,
I leave you, mark me, mark me now—
The sword of Bunker Hill.

"'Twas on that dread, immortal day,
I dared the Briton's band,
A captain raised this blade on me—
I tore it from his hand:
And while the glorious battle raged,
It lightened freedom's will—
For, boy, the God of freedom blessed
The sword of Bunker Hill.

"Oh, keep the sword!"—his accents broke—
A smile—and he was dead—
But his wrinkled hand still grasped the blade
Upon that dying bed.
The son remains; the sword remains—
Its glory growing still—
And twenty millions bless the sire,
And sword of Bunker Hill.

William Ross Wallace

# LIBERTY TREE[28]

## THOMAS PAINE

In a chariot of light from the regions of day,
The Goddess of Liberty came;
Ten thousand celestials directed the way,
And hither conducted the dame.
A fair budding branch from the gardens above,
Where millions with millions agree,
She brought in her hand as a pledge of her love,
And the plant she named *Liberty Tree.*

The celestial exotic struck deep in the ground,
Like a native it flourished and bore;
The fame of its fruit drew the nation's around,
To seek out this peaceable shore.
Unmindful of names or distinctions they came,
For freemen like brothers agree;
With one spirit endued, they one friendship pursued,
And their temple was *Liberty Tree.*

Beneath this fair tree, like the patriarchs of old,
Their bread in contentment they ate
Unvexed with the troubles of silver and gold,
The cares of the grand and the great.
With timber and tar they Old England supplied,
And supported her power on the sea;
Her battles they fought, without getting a groat,
For the honor of *Liberty Tree.*

But hear, O ye swains, 'tis a tale most profane,
How all the tyrannical powers,
Kings, Commons and Lords, are uniting amain,
To cut down this guardian of ours;
From the east to the west blow the trumpet to arms,
Through the land let the sound of it flee,
Let the far and the near, all unite with a cheer,
In defense of our *Liberty Tree.*

Thomas Paine

--------

[28] Published in the Pennsylvania Magazine, 1775.

# THE RISING IN 1776.[29]

## THOMAS BUCHANAN READ

Out of the North the wild news came,
Far flashing on its wings of flame,
Swift as the boreal light which flies
At midnight through the startled skies.
And there was tumult in the air,
The fife's shrill note, the drum's loud beat,
And through the wide land everywhere
The answering tread of hurrying feet;
While the first oath of Freedom's gun,
Came on the blast from Lexington;
And Concord, roused, no longer tame,
Forgot her old baptismal name,
Made bare her patriot arm of power,
And swelled the discord of the hour.

Within its shade of elm and oak
The church of Berkeley Manor stood;
There Sunday found the rural folk,
And some esteemed of gentle blood.
In vain their feet with loitering tread

[29] Used with the courteous permission of the publishers, The J. B. Lippincott Co.,
Philadelphia.

Passed 'mid the graves where rank is naught;
All could not read the lesson taught
In that republic of the dead.

How sweet the hour of Sabbath talk,
The vale with peace and sunshine full
Where all the happy people walk,
Decked in their homespun flax and wool!
Where youth's gay hats with blossoms bloom;
And every maid with simple art,
Wears on her breast, like her own heart,
A bud whose depths are all perfume;
While every garment's gentle stir
Is breathing rose and lavender.

The pastor came; his snowy locks
Hallowed his brow of thought and care;
And calmly, as shepherds lead their flocks,
He led into the house of prayer.
The pastor rose; the prayer was strong;
The psalm was warrior David's song;
The text, a few short words of might—
"The Lord of hosts shall arm the right!"

He spoke of wrongs too long endured,
Of sacred rights to be secured;
Then from his patriot tongue of flame
The startling words for Freedom came.
The stirring sentences he spake
Compelled the heart to glow or quake,
And, rising on his theme's broad wing,
And grasping in his nervous hand
The imaginary battle brand,
In face of death he dared to fling
Defiance to a tyrant king.

Even as he spoke, his frame, renewed
In eloquence of attitude,
Rose, as it seemed, a shoulder higher;
Then swept his kindling glance of fire
From startled pew to breathless choir;
When suddenly his mantle wide
His hands impatient flung aside,
And, lo! he met their wondering eyes
Complete in all a warrior's guise.

A moment there was awful pause—
When Berkeley cried, "Cease, traitor! cease!
God's temple is the house of peace!"

The other shouted, "Nay, not so,
When God is with our righteous cause;
His holiest places then are ours,
His temples are our forts and towers.
That frown upon the tyrant foe;
In this, the dawn of Freedom's day,
There is a time to fight and pray!"

And now before the open door—
The warrior priest had ordered so—
The enlisting trumpet's sudden roar
Rang through the chapel, o'er and o'er,
Its long reverberating blow,
So loud and clear, it seemed the ear
Of dusty death must wake and hear.
And there the startling drum and fife
Fired the living with fiercer life;
While overhead, with wild increase,
Forgetting its ancient toll of peace,
The great bell swung as ne'er before;
It seemed as it would never cease;
And every word its ardor flung
From off its jubilant iron tongue
Was, "War! War! War!"

"Who dares?"—this was the patriot's cry,
As striding from the desk he came—
"Come out with me, in Freedom's name,
For her to live, for her to die?"
A hundred hands flung up reply,
A hundred voices answered, "I!"

Thomas Buchanan Read

# AMERICA[30]

## BAYARD TAYLOR

Foreseen in the vision of sages,
Foretold when martyrs bled,
She was born of the longing of ages,
By the truth of the noble dead
And the faith of the living fed!
No blood in her lightest veins
Frets at remembered chains,
Nor shame of bondage has bowed her head.
In her form and features still
The unblenching Puritan will,
Cavalier honor, Huguenot grace,
The Quaker truth and sweetness,
And the strength of the danger-girdled race
Of Holland, blend in a proud completeness.

From the homes of all, where her being began,
She took what she gave to Man;
Justice, that knew no station,
Belief, as soul decreed,
Free air for aspiration,
Free force for independent deed!
She takes, but to give again,
As the sea returns the rivers in rain;
And gathers the chosen of her seed
From the hunted of every crown and creed.

Her Germany dwells by a gentler Rhine;
Her Ireland sees the old sunburst shine;
Her France pursues some dream divine;
Her Norway keeps his mountain pine;
Her Italy waits by the western brine;
And, broad-based under all,
Is planted England's oaken-hearted mood,
As rich in fortitude
As e'er went worldward from the island-wall!
Fused in her candid light,

[30] From the National Ode, July 4, 1876.

To one strong race all races here unite;
Tongues melt in hers, hereditary foemen
Forget their sword and slogan, kith and clan.
'Twas glory, once to be a Roman:
She makes it glory, now, to be a man!

Bayard Taylor

# THE BLUE AND THE GRAY
## FRANCIS MILES FINCH

By the flow of the inland river,
Whence the fleets of iron have fled,
Where the blades of the grave grass quiver,
Asleep are the ranks of the dead:
Under the sod and the dew,
Waiting the judgment day;
Under the one, the Blue,
Under the other, the Gray.

These in the robings of glory,
Those in the gloom of defeat,
All with the battle blood gory,
In the dusk of eternity meet:
Under the sod and the dew,
Waiting the judgment day;
Under the laurel, the Blue,
Under the willow, the Gray.

From the silence of sorrowful hours
The desolate mourners go,
Lovingly laden with flowers
Alike for the friend and the foe:
Under the sod and the dew,
Waiting the judgment day;
Under the roses, the Blue,
Under the lilies, the Gray.

So with an equal splendor
The morning sun rays fall,
With a touch impartially tender,
On the blossoms blooming for all:
Under the sod and the dew,
Waiting the judgment day;
Broidered with gold, the Blue,
Mellowed with gold, the Gray.

So, when the summer calleth,
On forest and field of grain,

With an equal murmur falleth
The cooling drip of the rain:
Under the sod and the dew,
Waiting the judgment day;
Wet with the rain, the Blue,
Wet with the rain, the Gray.

Sadly, but not with upbraiding,
The generous deed was done,
In the storm of the years that are fading,
No braver battle was won
Under the sod and the dew,
Waiting the judgment day;
Under the blossoms, the Blue,
Under the garlands, the Gray.

No more shall the war cry sever,
Or the winding rivers be red;
They banish our anger forever
When they laurel the graves of our dead!
Under the sod and the dew,
Waiting the judgment day;
Love and tears for the Blue,
Tears and love for the Gray.

Francis Miles Finch

# ABRAHAM LINCOLN[31]

## JAMES RUSSELL LOWELL

Life may be given in many ways,
And loyalty to Truth be sealed
As bravely in the closet as the field,
So bountiful is Fate;
But then to stand beside her,
When craven churls deride her,
To front a lie in arms and not to yield,
This shows, methinks, God's plan
And measure of a stalwart man,
Limbed like the old heroic breeds,
Who stand self-poised on manhood's solid earth,
Not forced to frame excuses for his birth,
Fed from within with all the strength he needs.
Such was he, our martyr chief,
Whom late the Nation he had led,
With ashes on her head,
Wept with the passion of an angry grief:
Forgive me, if from present things I turn
To speak what in my heart will beat and burn,
And hang my wreath on his world-honored urn.
Nature, they say, doth dote,
And cannot make a man
Save on some worn-out plan,
Repeating us by rote:
For him her Old-World molds aside she threw,
And, choosing sweet clay from the breast
Of the unexhausted West,
With stuff untainted shaped a hero new,
Wise, steadfast in the strength of God, and true.
How beautiful to see
Once more a shepherd of mankind indeed,
Who loved his charge, but never loved to lead;
One whose meek flock the people joyed to be,
Not lured by any cheat of birth,

[31] From the Ode recited at the Harvard Commemoration, July 21, 1865.

But by his clear-grained human worth,
And brave old wisdom of sincerity!
They knew that outward grace is dust;
They could not choose but trust
In that sure-footed mind's unfaltering skill,
And supple-tempered will
That bent like perfect steel to spring again and thrust.
His was no lonely mountain peak of mind,
Thrusting to thin air o'er our cloudy bars,
A sea mark now, now lost in vapor's blind;
Broad prairie rather, genial, level-lined,
Fruitful and friendly for all human kind,
Yet also nigh to Heaven and loved of loftiest stars.
Nothing of Europe here,
Or, then, of Europe fronting mornward still,
Ere any names of serf and peer
Could Nature's equal scheme deface
And thwart her genial will;
Here was a type of the true elder race,
And one of Plutarch's men talked with us face to face.
I praise him not; it were too late;
And some innative weakness there must be
In him who condescends to victory
Such as the Present gives, and cannot wait,
Safe in himself as in a fate.
So always firmly he:
He knew to bide his time,
And can his fame abide,
Still patient in his simple faith sublime,
Till the wise years decide.
Great captains, with their guns and drums,
Disturb our judgment for the hour,
But at last silence comes!
These all are gone, and standing like a tower,
Our children shall behold his fame,
The kindly-earnest, brave, foreseeing man,
Sagacious, patient, dreading praise, not blame,
New birth of our new soil, the first American.

James Russell Lowell

# THE FLAG GOES BY

## HENRY HOLCOMB BENNETT

Hats off!
Along the street there comes
A blare of bugles, a ruffle of drums,
A flash of color beneath the sky:
Hats off!
The flag is passing by!

Blue and crimson and white it shines,
Over the steel-tipped, ordered lines,
Hats off!
The colors before us fly;
But more than the flag is passing by.

Sea fights and land fights, grim and great,
Fought to make and save the State:
Weary marches and sinking ships;
Cheers of victory on dying lips;

Days of plenty and years of peace;
March of a strong land's swift increase;
Equal justice, right, and law,
Stately honor and reverend awe;

Sign of a nation, great and strong
To ward her people from foreign wrong:
Pride and glory and honor—all
Live in the colors to stand or fall.
Hats off!
Along the street there comes
A blare of bugles, a ruffle of drums;
And loyal hearts are beating high:
Hats off!
The flag is passing by!

Henry Holcomb Bennett

# THE SHIP OF STATE

## HENRY WADSWORTH LONGFELLOW

Thou, too, sail on, O Ship of State!
Sail on, O Union, strong and great!
Humanity with all its fears,
With all the hopes of future years,
Is hanging breathless on thy fate!
We know what Master laid thy keel,
What Workmen wrought thy ribs of steel,
Who made each mast, and sail, and rope,
What anvils rang, what hammers beat,
In what a forge and what a heat
Were shaped the anchors of thy hope!
Fear not each sudden sound and shock,
'Tis of the wave and not the rock;
'Tis but the flapping of the sail,
And not a rent made by the gale!
In spite of rock and tempest's roar
In spite of false lights on the shore,
Sail on, nor fear to breast the sea!
Our hearts, our hopes, are all with thee,
Our hearts, our hopes, our prayers, our tears,
Our faith triumphant o'er our fears,
Are all with thee—are all with thee!

Henry Wadsworth Longfellow

# THE NAME OF OLD GLORY[32]

## JAMES WHITCOMB RILEY

Old Glory! say who,
By the ships and the crew,
And the long, blended ranks of the grey and the blue—
Who gave you, Old Glory, the name that you bear
With such pride everywhere
As you cast yourself free to the rapturous air
And leap out full length as we're wanting you to?
Who gave you that name, with the ring of the same,
And the honor and fame so becoming to you?—
Your stripes streaked in ripples of white and of red,
With your stars at their glittering best overhead—
By day or by night,
Their delightfulest light
Laughing down from their little square heaven of blue!
Who gave you the name of Old Glory?—say who—
Who gave you the name of Old Glory?

The old banner lifted, and faltering then,
In vague lisps and whispers fell silent again.

Old Glory,—speak out!—we are asking about
How you happened to "favor" a name, so to say,
That sounds so familiar and careless and gay
As we cheer it and shout in our wild, breezy way—
We—the *crowd*, every man of us, calling you that—
We—Tom, Dick and Harry—each swinging his hat—
And hurrahing "Old Glory," like you were our kind,
When—Lord—we all know we're as common as sin!

And yet it just seems like you *humor* us all
And waft us your thanks as we hail you and fall
Into line, with you over us, waving us on
Where our glorified, sanctified betters have gone—
And this is the reason we're wanting to know—
(And we're wanting it so!
Where our own fathers went, we are willing to go)

[32] From the Biographical Edition of the Complete Works of James Whitcomb Riley.
Copyright 1913. Used by special permission of the publishers, The Bobbs-Merrill Company.

Who gave you the name of Old Glory—Oho!
Who gave you the name of Old Glory?

The old flag unfurled in a billowy thrill
For an instant, then wistfully sighed and was still.

Old Glory—the story we're wanting to hear
Is what the plain facts of your christening were—
For your name—just to hear it,
Repeat it, and cheer it, 's a tang to the spirit
As salt as a tear;—
And seeing you fly, and the boys marching by,
There's a shout in the throat and a blur in the eye
And an aching to live for you always—or die,
If, dying, we still keep you waving on high.
And so, by our love
For you, floating above,
And the scars of all wars and the sorrows thereof,
Who gave you the name of Old Glory, and why
Are we thrilled at the name of Old Glory?
Then the old banner leaped, like a sail in the blast,
And fluttered an audible answer at last.

And it spake, with a shake of the voice, and it said:—
By the driven snow-white and the living blood-red
Of my bars, and their heaven of stars overhead—
By the symbol conjoined of them all, skyward cast,
As I float from the steeple, or flap at the mast,
Or droop o'er the sod where the long grasses nod,—
My name is as old as the glory of God,
... So I came by the name of Old Glory.

James Whitcomb Riley

Lector House believes that a society develops through a two-fold approach of continuous learning and adaptation, which is derived from the study of classic literary works spread across the historic timeline of literature records. Therefore, we aim at reviving, repairing and redeveloping all those inaccessible or damaged but historically as well as culturally important literature across subjects so that the future generations may have an opportunity to study and learn from past works to embark upon a journey of creating a better future.

This book is a result of an effort made by Lector House towards making a contribution to the preservation and repair of original ancient works which might hold historical significance to the approach of continuous learning across subjects.

**HAPPY READING & LEARNING!**

**LECTOR HOUSE LLP**
**E-MAIL: lectorpublishing@gmail.com**